I0795935

POSTCARD HISTORY SERIES

Wyoming County

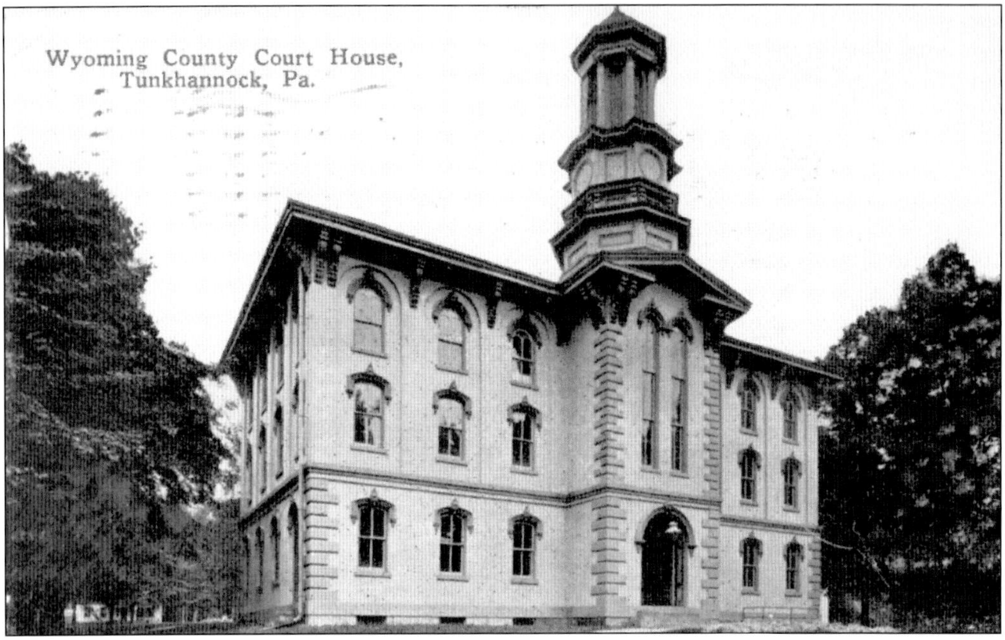

The Wyoming County Courthouse was originally built in 1843, one year after the county was formed out of Luzerne County. The original building, which cost $5,000 to build, has been remodeled numerous times. This card is postmarked August 11, 1913, and was sent to Maryland.

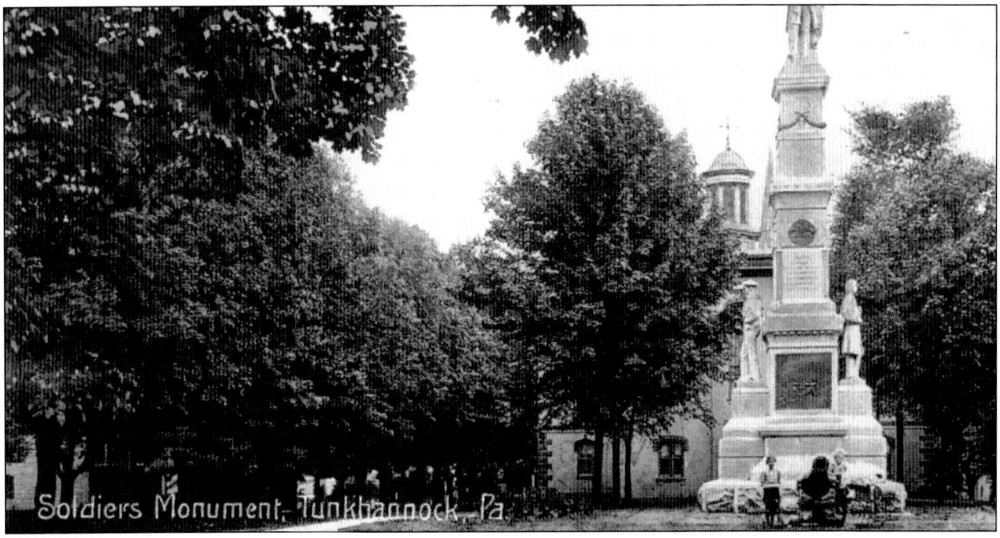

This 39-foot, 72-ton granite monument, which sits behind the courthouse, was dedicated on October 19, 1897, in memory of the soldiers and sailors from Wyoming County who fought for the preservation of the Union. This card is postmarked 1910.

POSTCARD HISTORY SERIES

Wyoming County

Sean and Johanna S. Billings

ARCADIA
PUBLISHING

ISBN 978-0-7385-3491-6

Published by Arcadia Publishing
Charleston, South Carolina

Library of Congress Catalog Card Number: 2003114168

For all general information, contact Arcadia Publishing:
Telephone 843-853-2070
Fax 843-853-0044
E-mail sales@arcadiapublishing.com
For customer service and orders:
Toll-Free 1-888-313-2665

Visit us on the Internet at www.arcadiapublishing.com

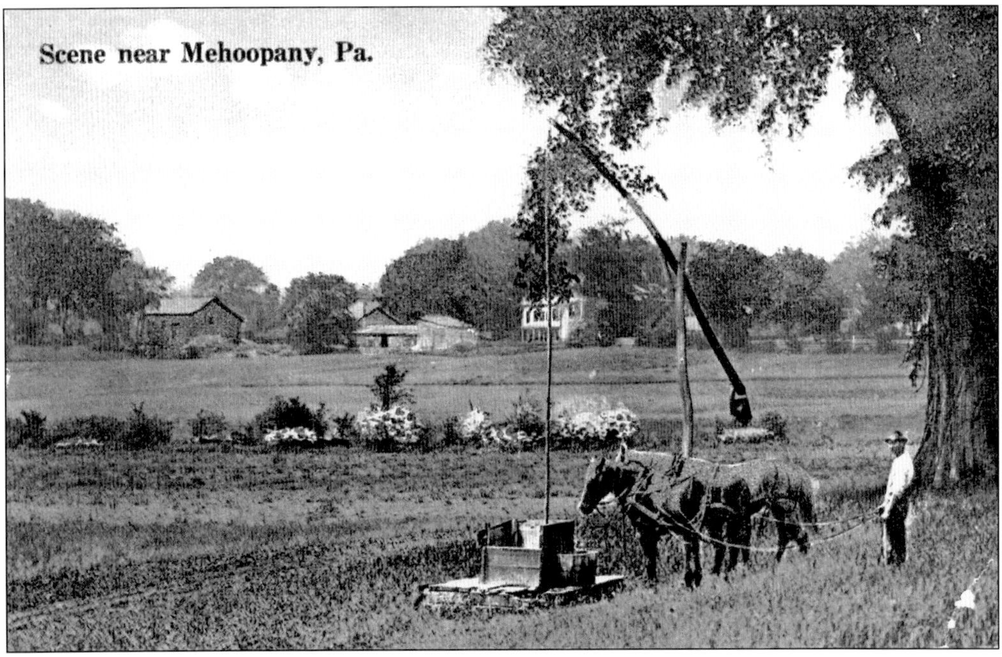

Farming was a way of life in Wyoming County, where most people produced their own food.

Contents

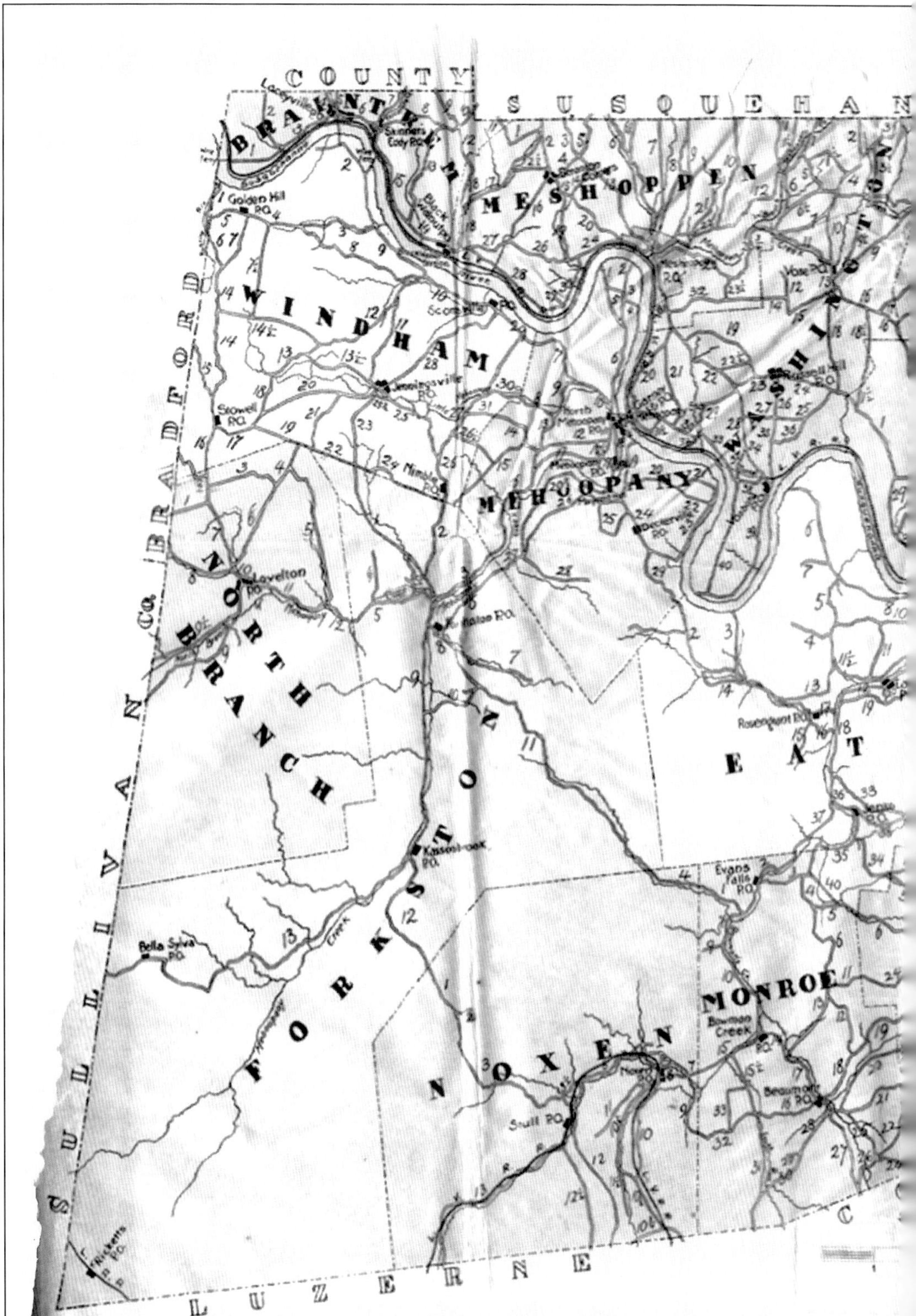
COUNTY
BRAINTRIM
MESHOPPEN
WASHINGTON
WINDHAM
MEHOOPANY
NORTH BRANCH
FORKSTON
EATON
MONROE
NOXEN
SUSQUEHAN
BRADFORD Co.
SULLIVAN
LUZERNE
Golden Hill P.O.
Stowell P.O.
Jenningsville P.O.
Scottsville P.O.
Lovelton P.O.
Bella Sylva P.O.
Kasson P.O.
Evans Falls P.O.
Bowman Creek P.O.
Beaumont P.O.
Stull P.O.
Ricketts P.O.
Vose P.O.
Rosengrant P.O.

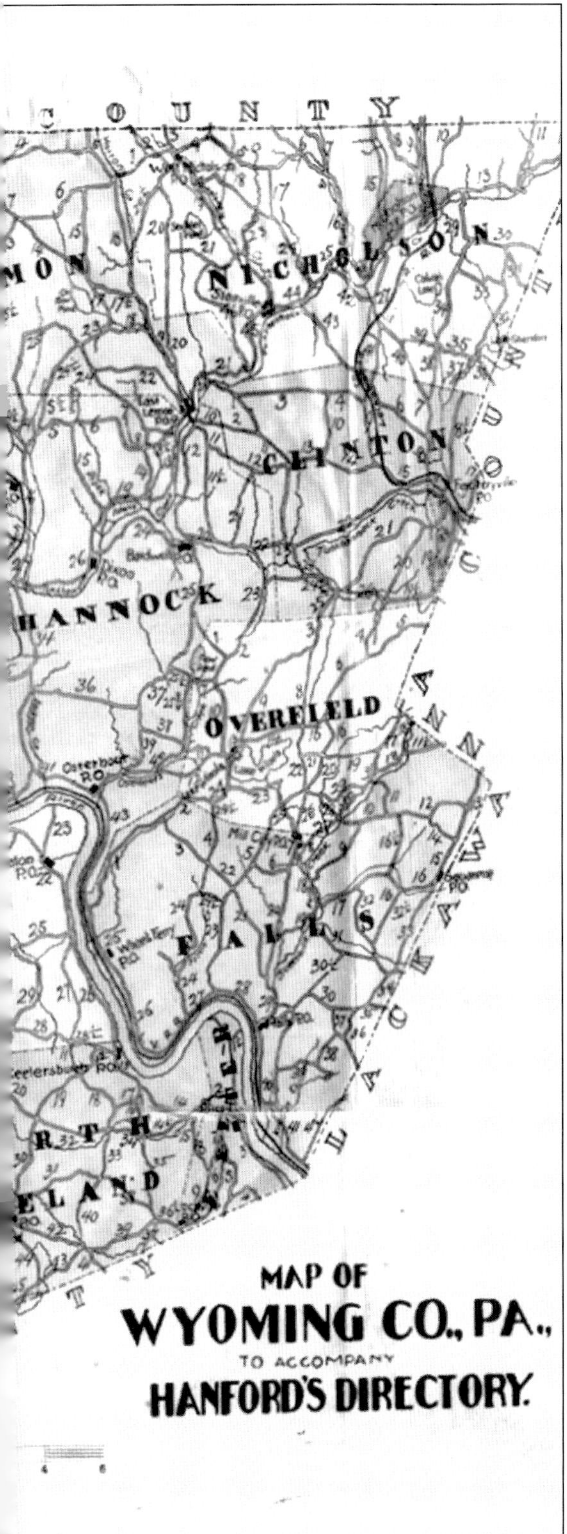

This map appears in the *1900 Hanford's Directory of Wyoming County.*

To Harold Alfred Ray, Beatrice Lacey Williams Ray,
Allison Bertram Major, and Mary Virginia Rosser Major.

INTRODUCTION

Wyoming County was formed out of Luzerne County on April 4, 1842, by an act of the Pennsylvania legislature. The original petition asked that the county be called Putnam after Revolutionary War general Israel Putnam, but the name Wyoming was substituted in honor of the Wyoming Valley. The name Wyoming is derived from an American Indian word meaning "extensive meadows."

Wyoming County is one of the four counties that made up the historic Wyoming Valley. Many of the early settlers came to the area from Connecticut, and by the 1750s, this influx had begun to cause friction between Pennsylvania and Connecticut. The tension resulted in the Yankee-Pennamite Wars in which both Pennsylvania and Connecticut claimed control of northeastern Pennsylvania.

Wyoming County includes five boroughs—Factoryville, Laceyville, Meshoppen, Nicholson, and Tunkhannock—and 18 townships—Braintrim, Clinton, Eaton, Exeter, Falls, Forkston, Lemon, Mehoopany, Meshoppen, Monroe, Nicholson, North Branch, Northmoreland, Noxen, Overfield, Tunkhannock, Washington, and Windham.

The first courthouse for the new county was built in Tunkhannock in 1843. It was 40 feet square and two stories high. In 1869, the courthouse was repaired and a front was added to it. The front measured 76 by 40 feet and was three stories high. The rear was expanded to 70 by 70 feet at this time. The courthouse was renovated from 1978 to 1979 and again in the 1990s.

The first jail, built in 1843, was located 150 feet behind the courthouse and had four cells. In 1866, a new jail was constructed of stone with a brick jailer's residence in front. The jail was 33 by 35 feet and had six cells. On May 4, 1985, this jail was removed and a new jail was built.

In 1852, the first boat passed through the North Branch Extension Canal, built along the Susquehanna River, connecting Northumberland to Sayre, New York. The canal was heavily damaged in the flood of 1865 and was closed in 1872. Three of the nine locks in Wyoming County were located in Meshoppen, and the other six were at McKune, Jenkins, Tunkhannock, Horse Race, Black Walnut, and Laceyville. The county also included 11 canal aqueducts, the longest being 337 feet across the Tunkhannock Creek. To raise the water level to fill the canal, a dam was built at Horse Race, behind what is now Proctor & Gamble. Some of the wooden cribbing and iron spikes used to build the dam can still be seen when the water level is low.

A number of railroads also crossed the county. In 1868, the Lehigh Valley Railroad was completed along the eastern side of the river to a point one mile below Tunkhannock. In 1870, the bridge across the Tunkhannock Creek was constructed, completing the railroad to Waverly, New York. The railroad was double tracked in Wyoming County by 1890.

In 1871, construction began for the Montrose Railway, which ran from Tunkhannock to Montrose. It was constructed as a narrow-gauge railroad three feet in width. By 1876, when the railroad was finished, the Lehigh Valley owned it and operated it as a narrow-gauge railroad until 1904, when it was converted to standard gauge.

By 1892, the Lehigh Valley Railroad built the Bowman's Creek Branch, which ran from Noxen to Wilkes-Barre through Harvey's Lake in Luzerne County. In 1892, tracks were built to connect Noxen with Ricketts through Stull and Mountain Springs. This railroad was used mostly for hauling lumber and, later, for hauling ice from the harvesting operations in Mountain Springs, west of Noxen. Service from Noxen to Luzerne County was discontinued on December 22, 1963, and the railroad tracks and structures were removed by the end of 1964.

The Delaware, Lackawanna & Western Railroad ran through Factoryville and Nicholson across the famous Tunkhannock Viaduct.

The economy of Wyoming County was driven by lumbering until 1900. The lumber industry spawned the leather-tanning industry because it provided hemlock bark needed for tanning. Around the turn of the century, dairy farming replaced lumber as the main industry in the county. Stone quarrying, especially Pennsylvania Bluestone, increased over this time also.

In 1966, the Charmin Paper Company, now Procter & Gamble, opened in Mehoopany and is now the county's largest employer.

One

The County Seat

Tunkhannock Township traces its origins back to the Connecticut claims of pre–Revolutionary War times. After the Wyoming Massacre in 1778, Connecticut settlers fled to safer locations, including Dutchess County, New York. In 1786, settlers returned to the area and it was named Tunkhannock. The name, which was spelled either Tunkhannunk or Tonkhonink, is an American Indian word meaning "two small streams of water falling into one another, opposite of each other." The two streams are Bowman's Creek and Tunkhannock Creek, both of which flow into the Susquehanna River.

Among the original Connecticut settlers to return to the area to reestablish the township were members of the Billings, Bowen, Braton, Marcy, Slocum, and Tripp families.

The borough of Tunkhannock was organized in 1841, and the first post office was opened in 1801 with Isaac Slocum as postmaster.

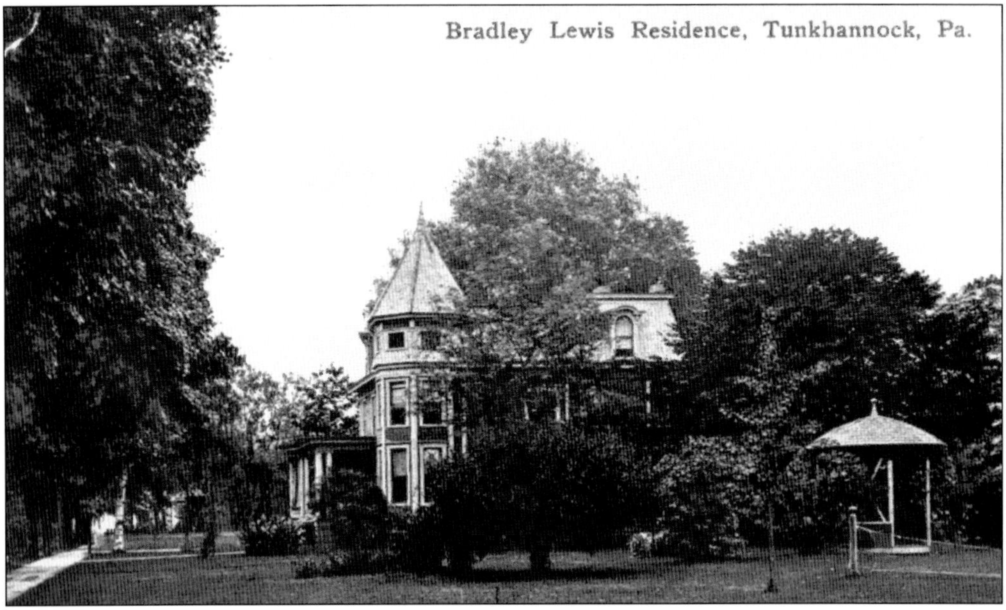

This Victorian house, identified on this postcard as the home of Bradley Lewis, is typical of the large beautiful homes that grace the streets of Tunkhannock.

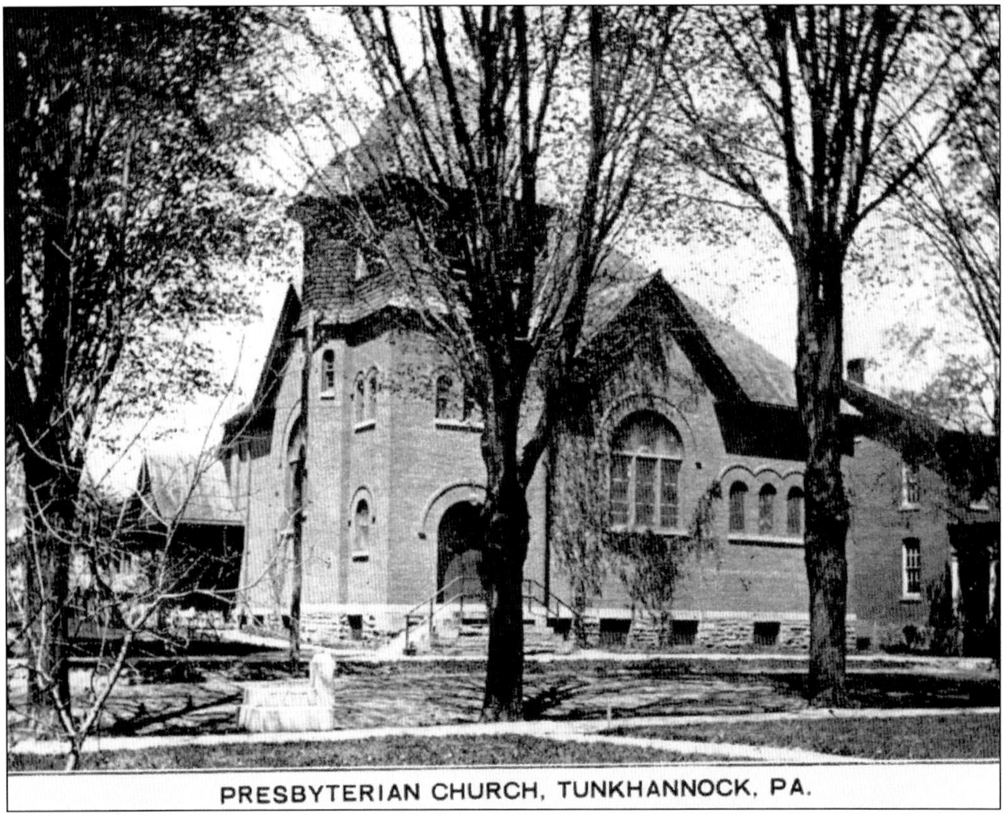

This postcard shows the second building, constructed in 1891, that was used by the Presbyterian church located on Putnam Street. The first building was destroyed by fire.

The Tunkhannock Methodist Episcopal Church, shown here, was built in 1868 and was destroyed by fire in 1937. A new church was built and dedicated in 1939. The card is postmarked 1910.

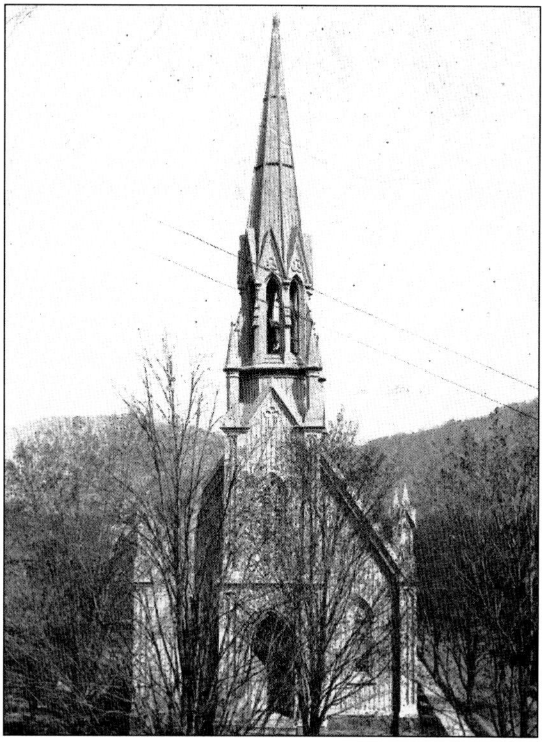

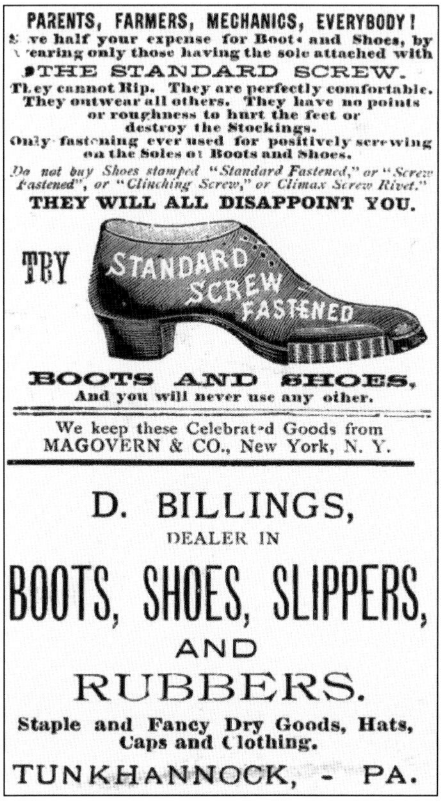

This advertising card promotes shoes for sale by Draper Billings, who had a three-story brick store on Bridge Street. After 1911, Draper's nephew ran Billings Furniture and Undertaking in the same building, which was destroyed by fire in 1991.

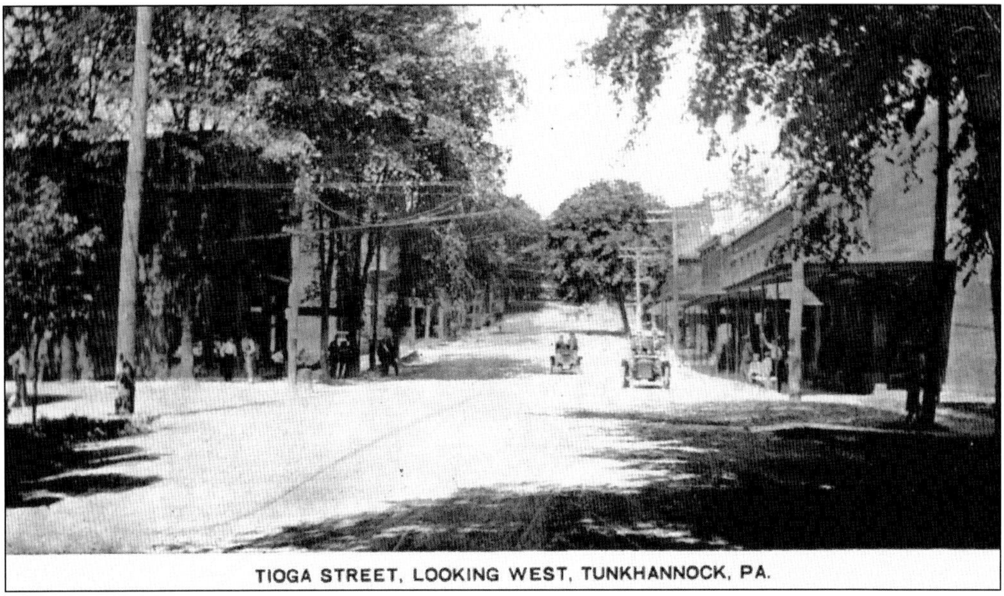

Notice the cars in this view of Tioga Street, looking west. You can no longer read the postmark, but the style of the handwriting on the back, the appearance of the cars, the dirt street, and the trees all indicate this card dates from the early part of the 20th century.

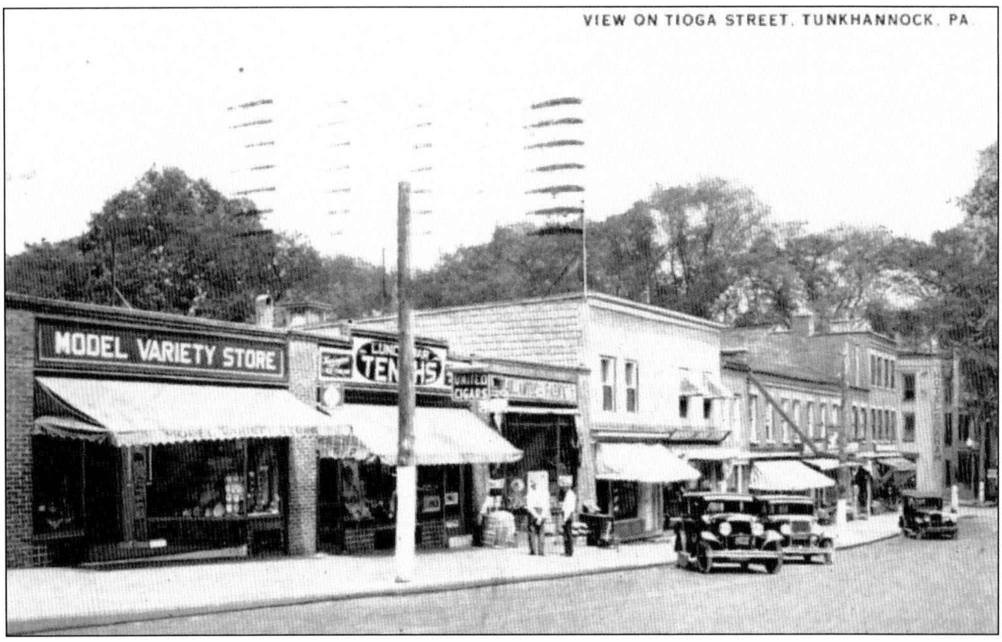

You can see the Hotel Graham to the right in this *c.* 1934 view looking down Tioga Street to the south.

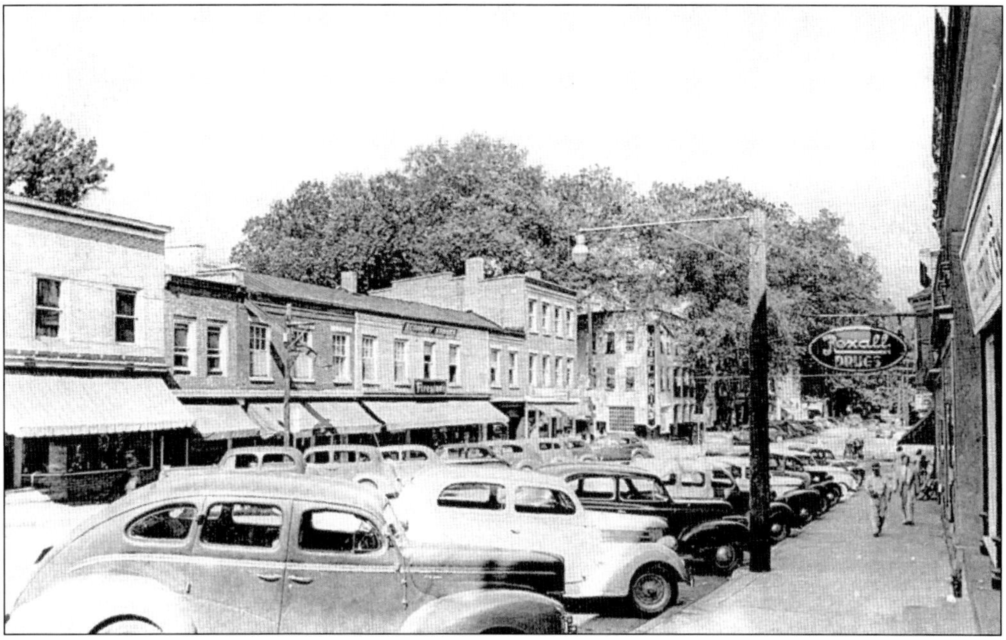

This *c.* 1940s view of Tioga Street includes the Hotel Prins, which later became known as the Prince Hotel.

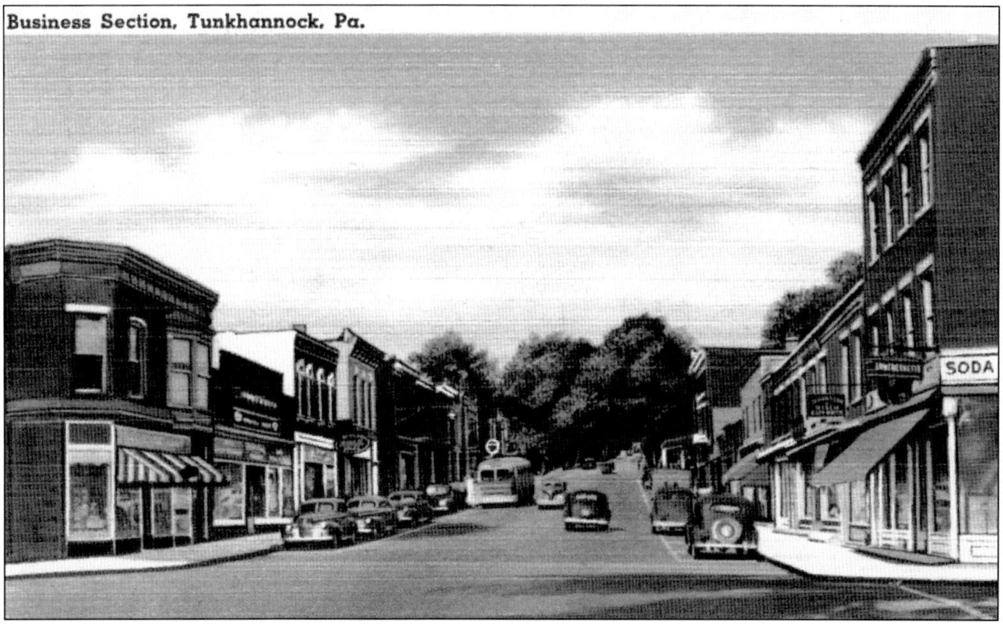

In this *c.* 1940s view, looking up Tioga Street, cars are parallel parked rather than parked head in and at an angle, as they had been in the past.

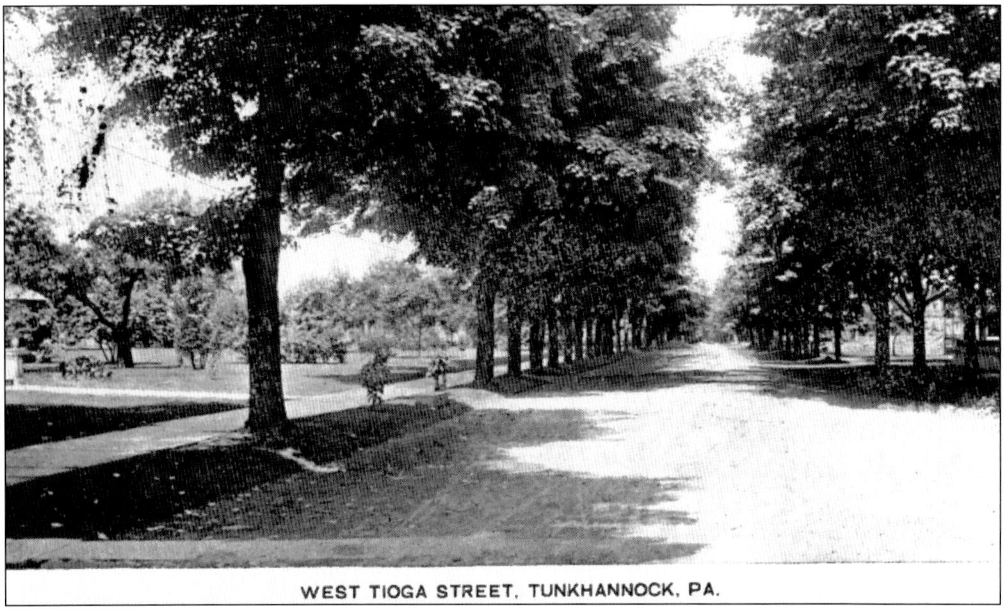

The postmark on this card, showing West Tioga Street, is 1909. The road appears to be dirt.

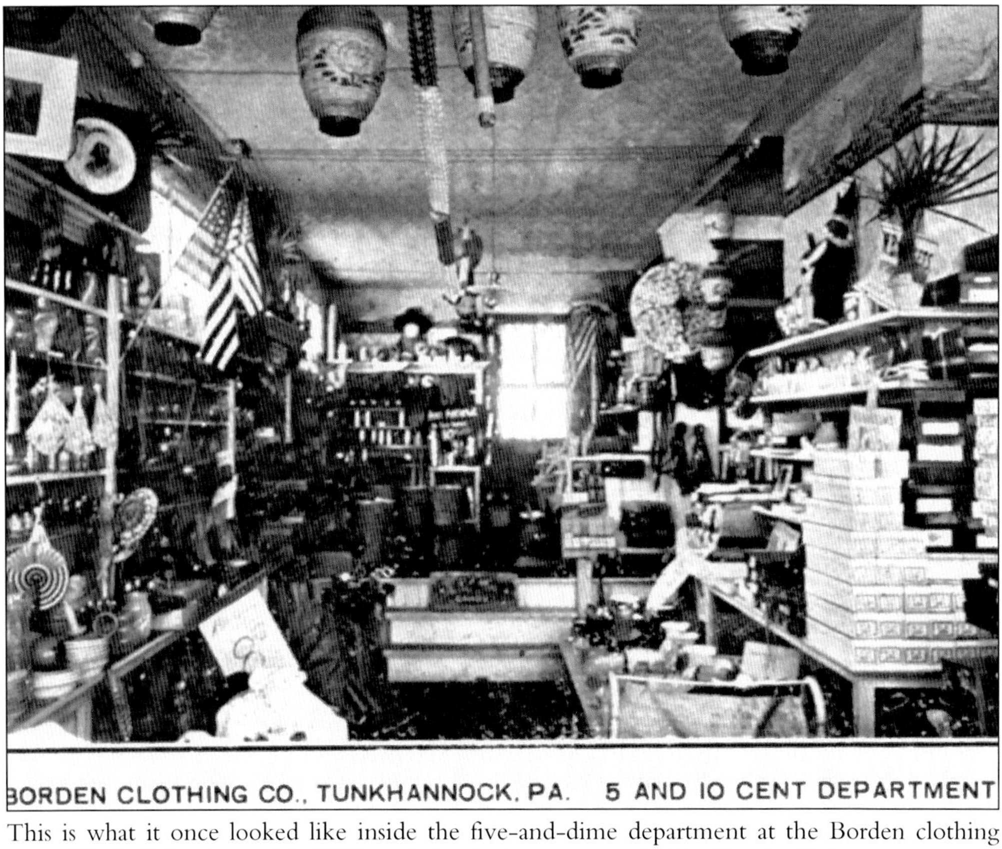

This is what it once looked like inside the five-and-dime department at the Borden clothing store. The building burned in 1910, and the site is now occupied by Beagles Pub.

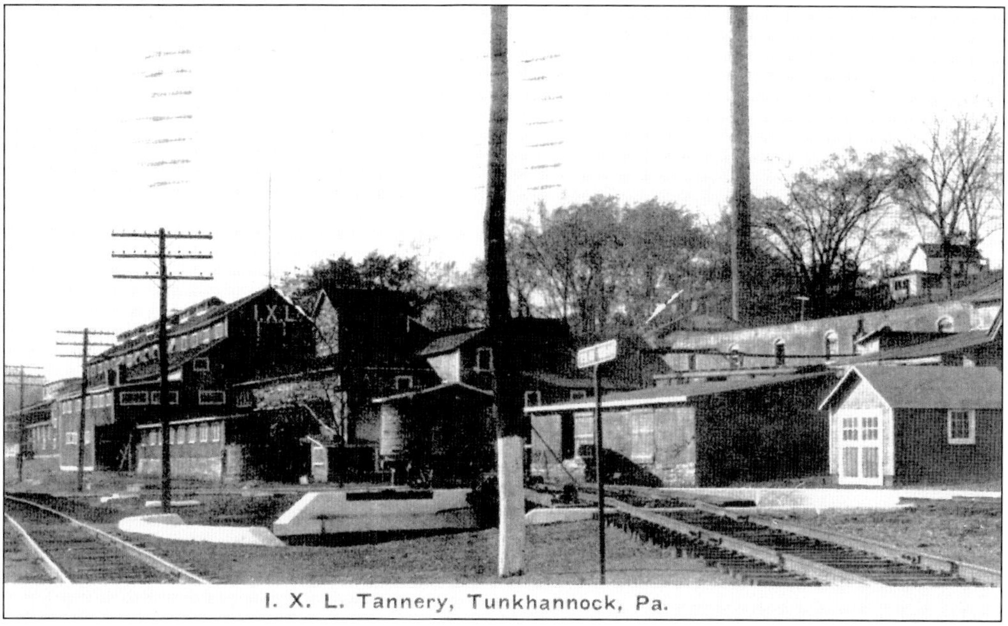

The I.X.L. Tannery, shown here on a card postmarked 1934, was located along the railroad tracks in town. It was built in 1866 and remained in operation until the early 1930s. The Tunkhannock Bypass now covers most of the area where the tannery was located.

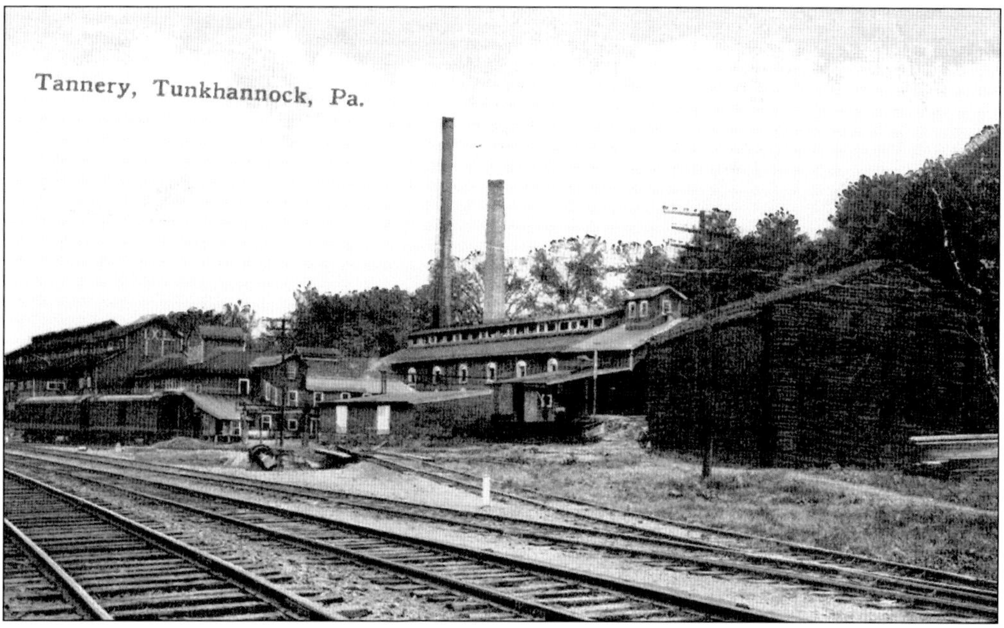

During its operation, the I.X.L. Tannery, shown here as it looked around the beginning of the 20th century, was the largest employer in Wyoming County. The tannery used 60,000 tons of bark annually from Pennsylvania's state tree, the eastern hemlock, to process more than 30,000 hides. Hemlock bark is an excellent source of the tannic acid needed to tan animal hides.

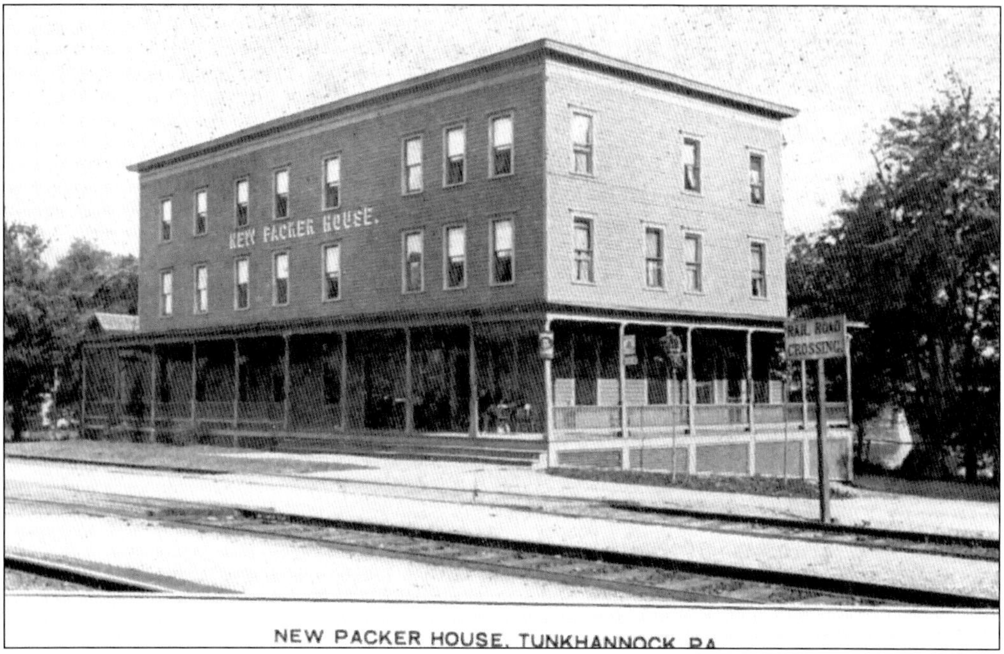

The Packer House was built in 1872 to serve passengers of the Lehigh Valley Railroad. It was rebuilt after being destroyed by fire in 1900, but it was not rebuilt after another fire destroyed the newer building in 1919.

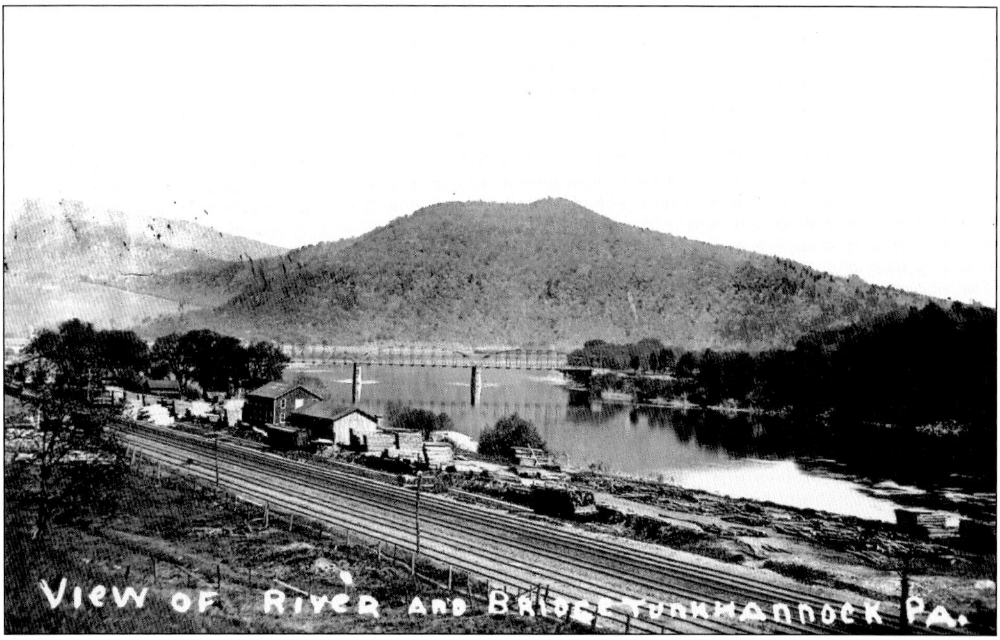

This *c.* 1908 view shows the Lehigh Valley Railroad, the Susquehanna River, and the bridge. Built in 1903, this was the second bridge to cross the river at this location.

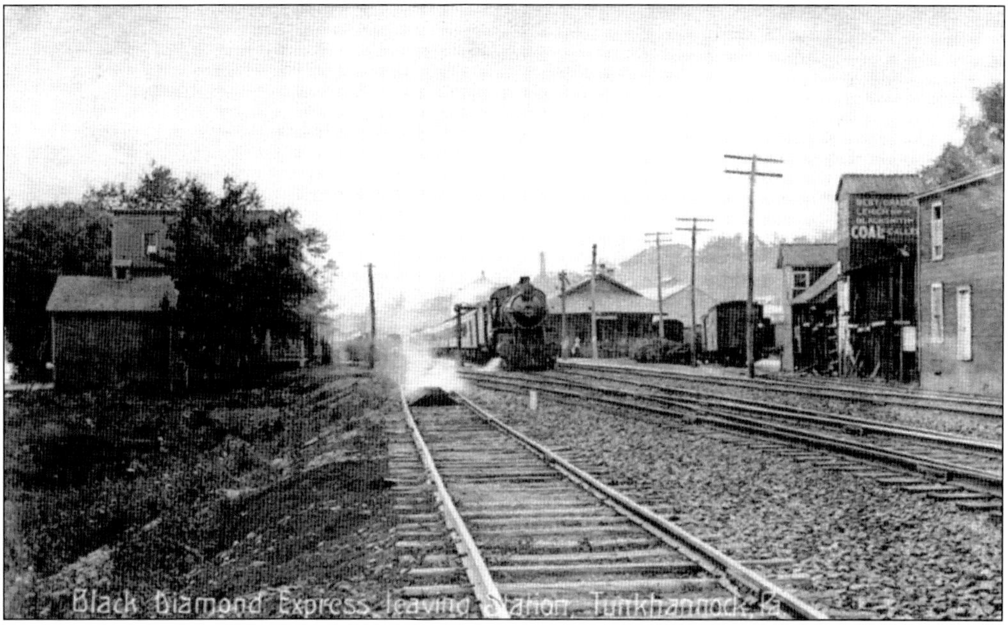

The Lehigh Valley Railroad's *Black Diamond Express* was started in 1896 and was touted as "the Handsomest Train in the World." The *Express,* shown here in Tunkhannock, ran daily except for Sunday and made its Jersey City–Buffalo trip in just under 10 hours.

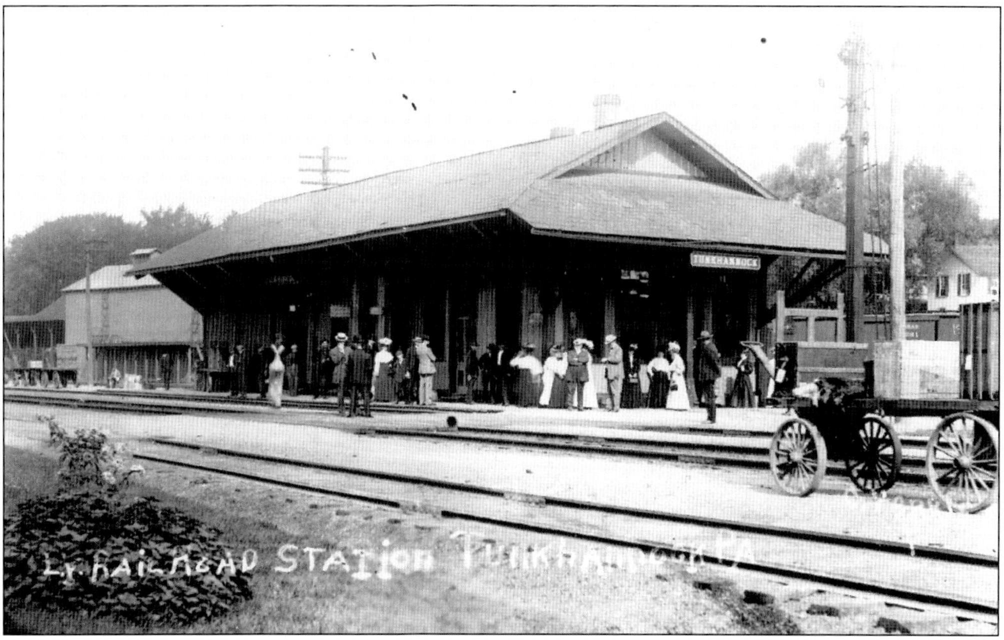

The Lehigh Valley Railroad station in Tunkhannock is shown in this photo postcard, which dates from the beginning of the 20th century.

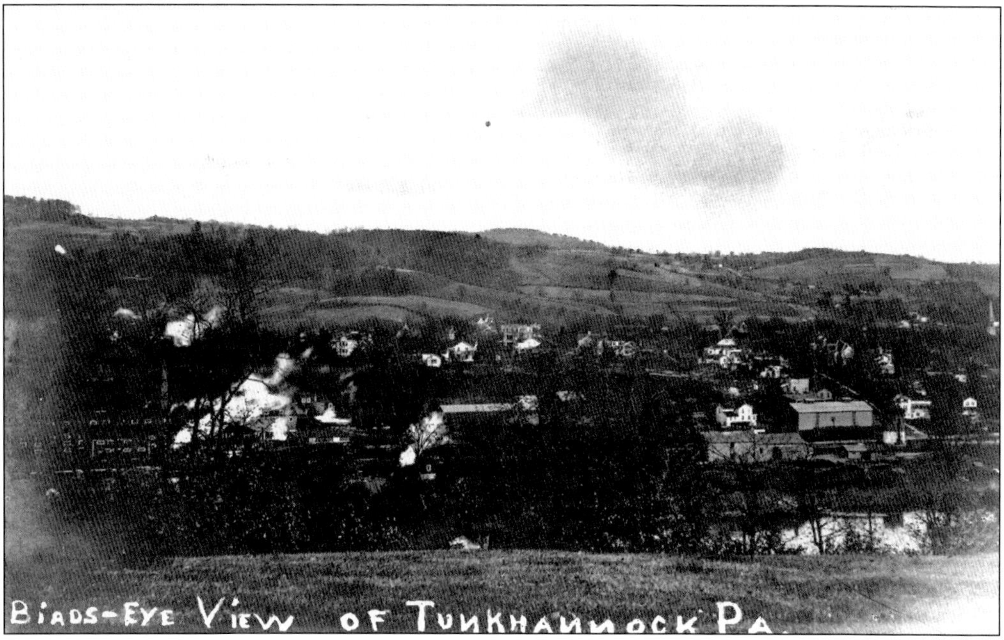

This bird's-eye view shows Tunkhannock from across the Susquehanna River.

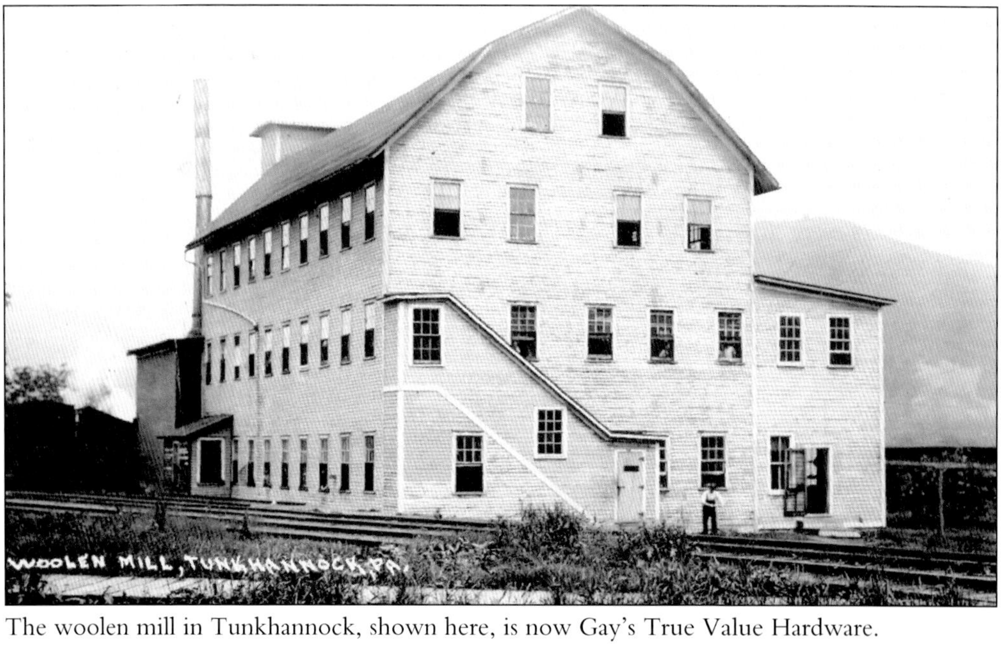

The woolen mill in Tunkhannock, shown here, is now Gay's True Value Hardware.

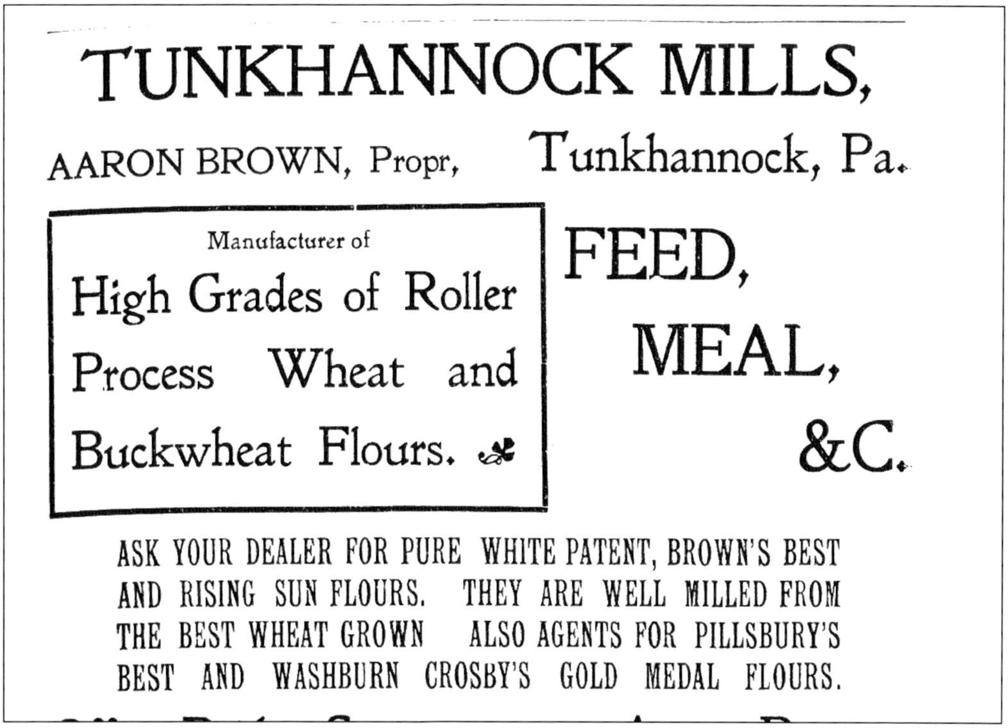

This advertisement for the Tunkhannock Mills appears in the *1900 Hanford's Directory of Wyoming County*. The company had offices on Bridge Street and was owned by Aaron Brown. Brown had a home on East Tioga Street, but the building no longer stands.

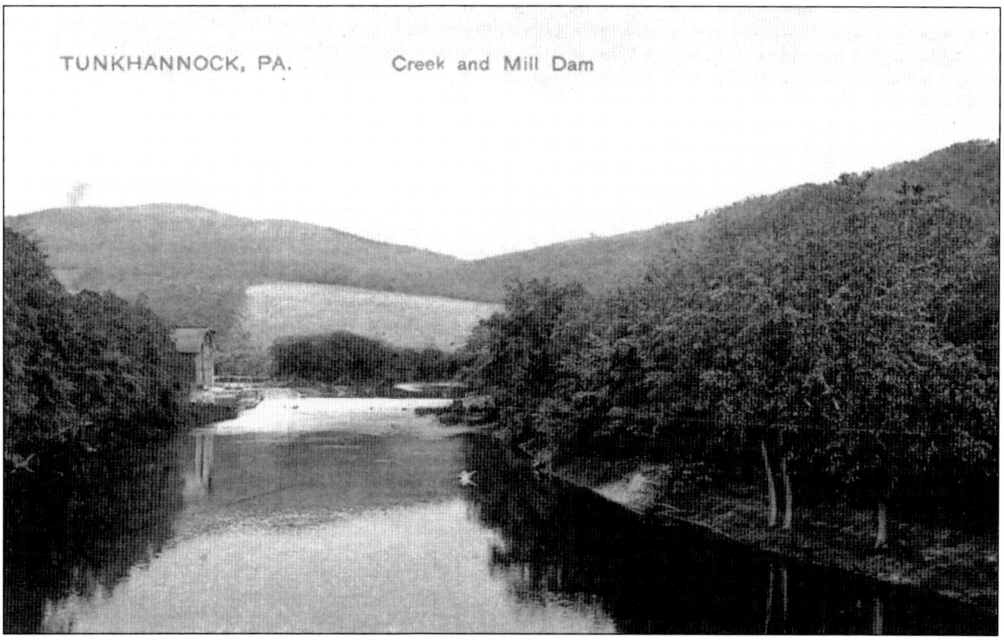

The Tunkhannock Creek was good source of water for milling operations and was dammed to provide the waterpower. The view here is of Brown's Mill.

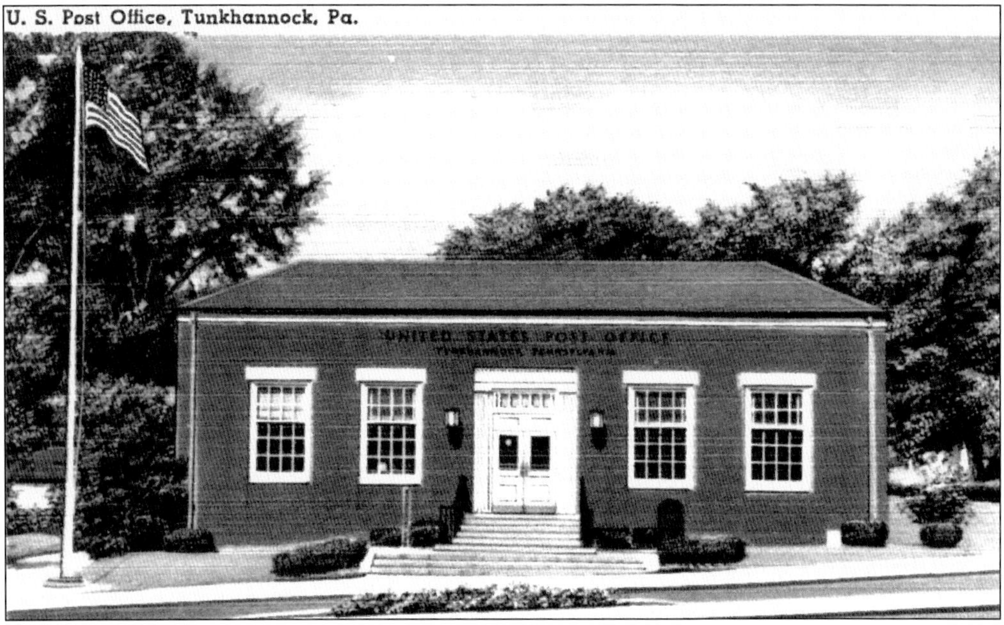

Peter Ace's blacksmith shop on Bridge Street was removed so that the current Tunkhannock post office, shown here, could be built in 1938.

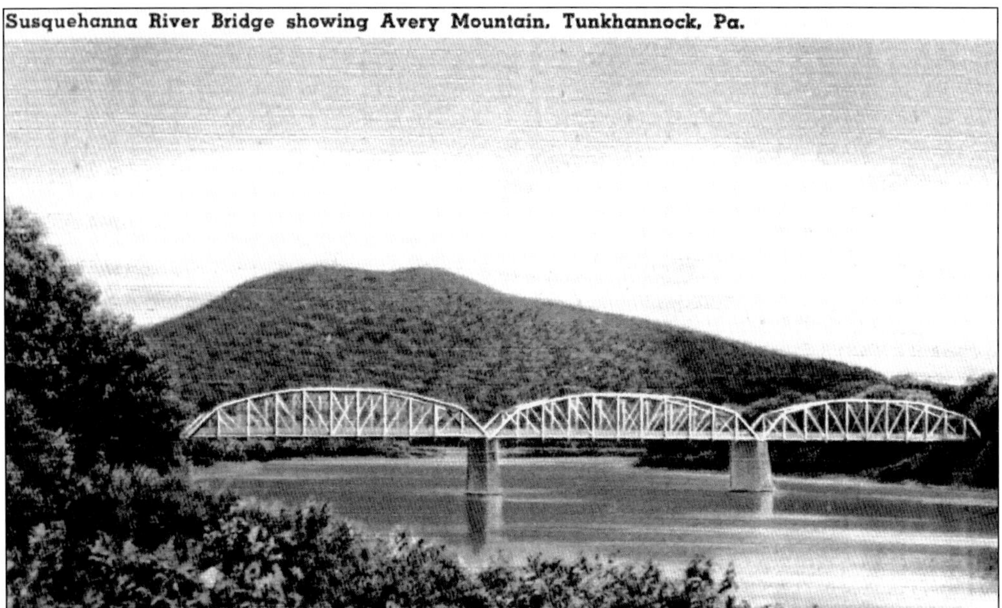

Built in 1903, this bridge was damaged in the flood of 1972 and was removed in 1980 after the current bridge was built. The first bridge at this location was a covered bridge that was damaged by a flood in 1902.

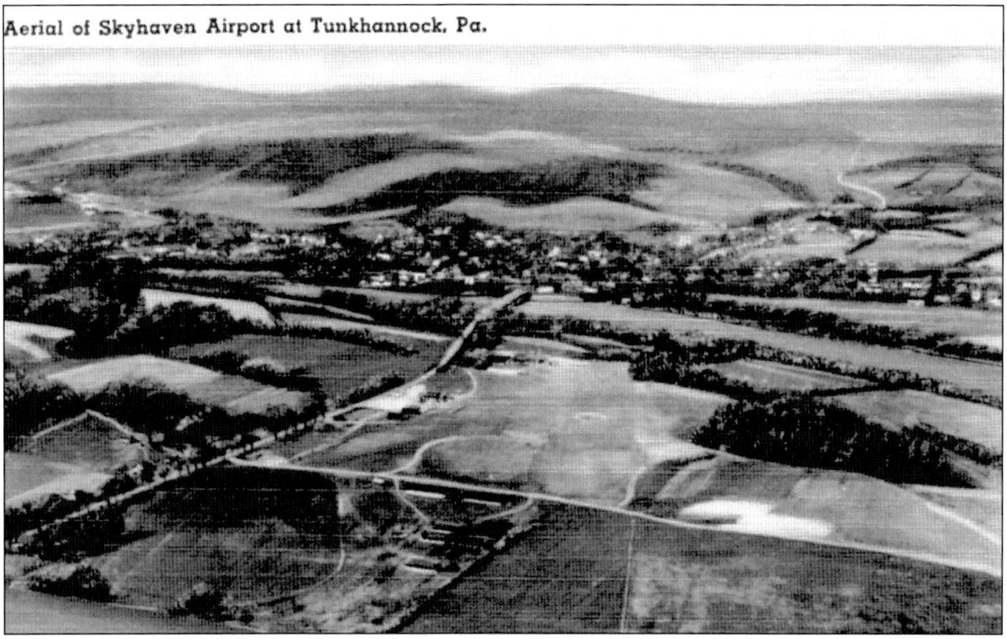

The Skyhaven Airport was started in 1945 by Charles Gay and Alvah Fassett. The only commercial airport in the county, it had a grass runway until 1991, when the runway was paved.

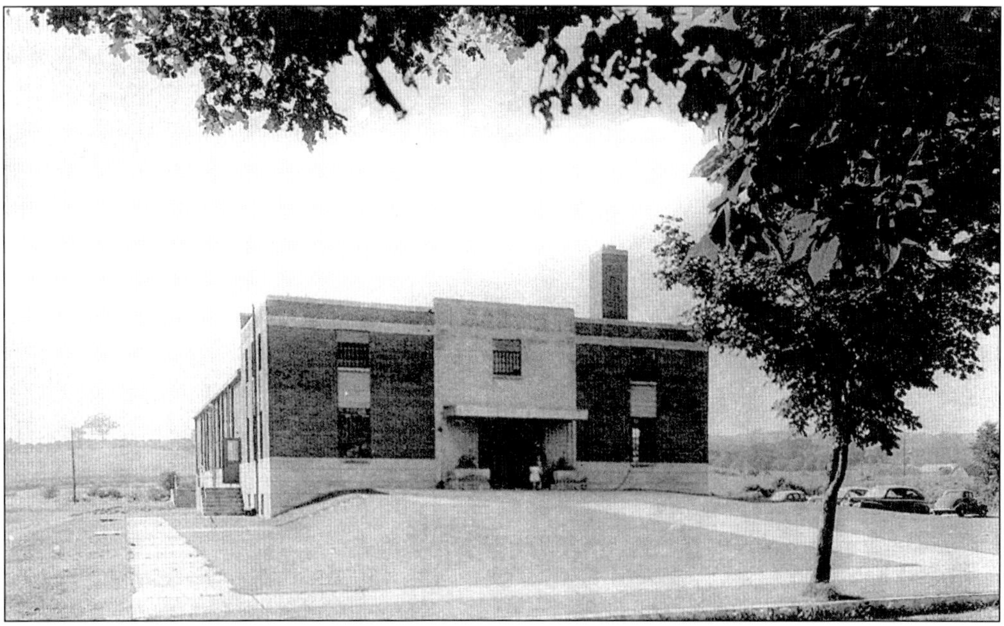

The armory on West Street became the home of the National Guard 109th Company B in 1938. The building was leased to the Endicott Johnson Shoe Company in 1945, after Company B was called to active duty. In 1980, Endicott Johnson bought the building. Sometime during the 1980s, when the shoe company stopped making shoes there, the building was sold to the Ace-Robbins Oil Company. It is now home to the Eastern Pennsylvania Supply Company (EPSCO).

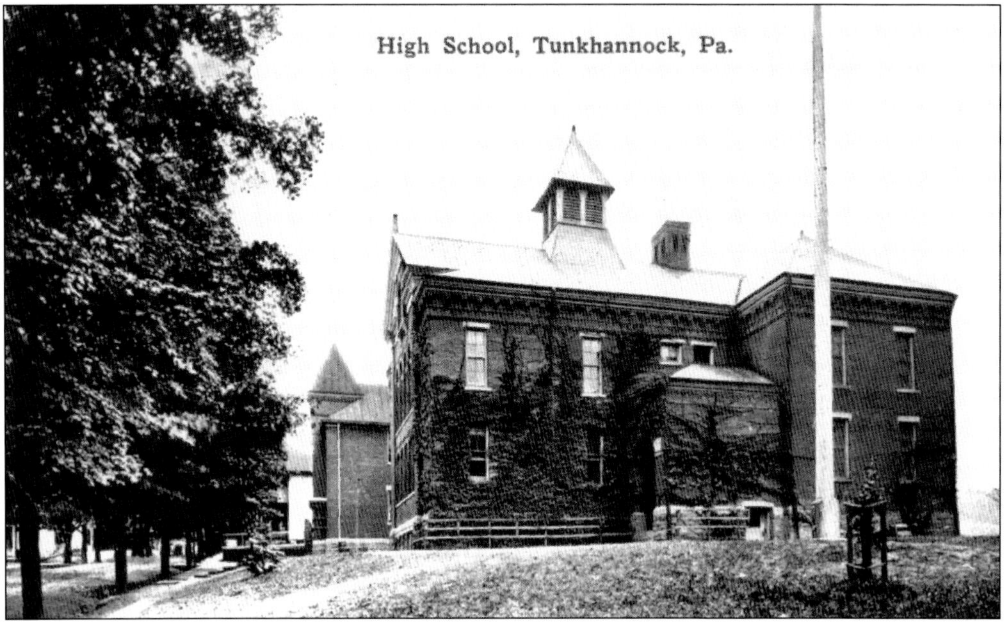

The Harrison Street School was built in 1855 and was used as a school until 1971. The building has housed the Wyoming County Historical Society since 1981.

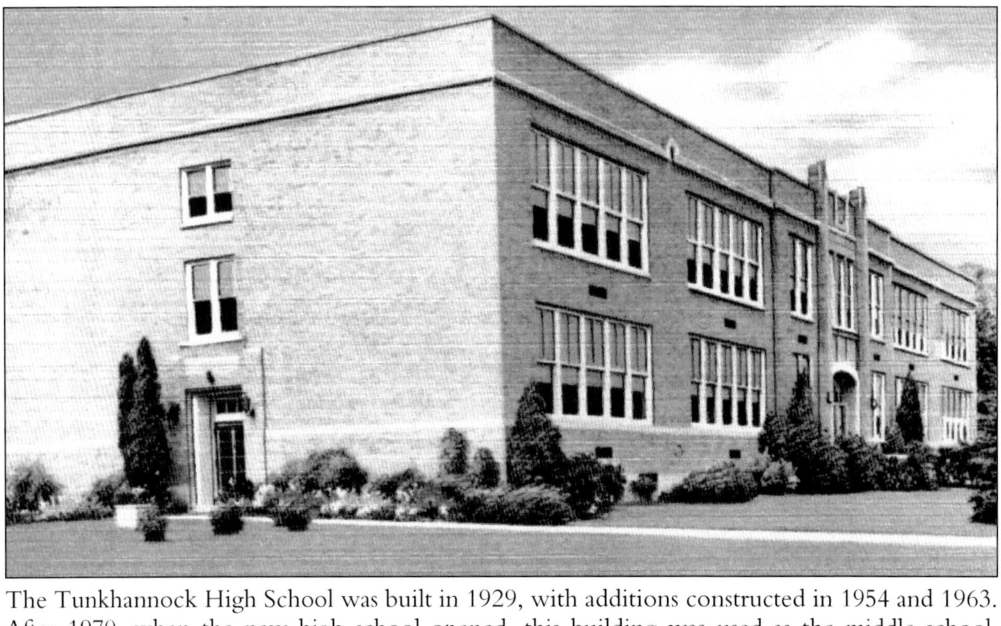

The Tunkhannock High School was built in 1929, with additions constructed in 1954 and 1963. After 1970, when the new high school opened, this building was used as the middle school, housing grades six through eight. Most of the school was demolished in 1999, when the new middle school was built. A portion of the building has been converted into the Tunkhannock Area School District Central Administration offices.

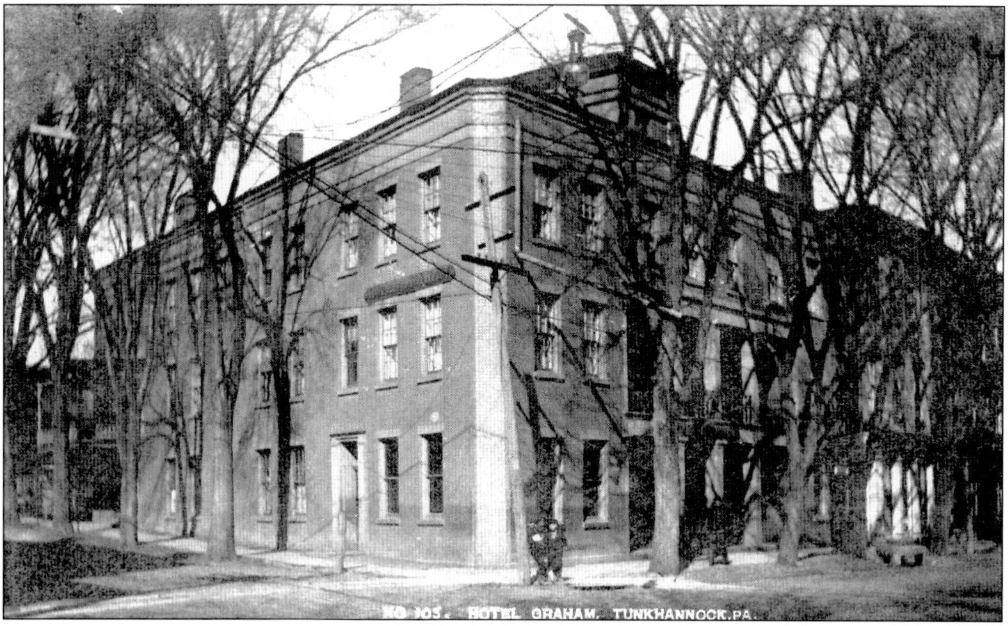

The Hotel Graham was originally called the American House and was built in 1844 by Henry Stark. It was sold to Thomas Wall in 1860 and renamed Wall's Hotel. In 1890, DeWitt C. Graham purchased the hotel and renamed it the Hotel Graham. This card is postmarked 1908.

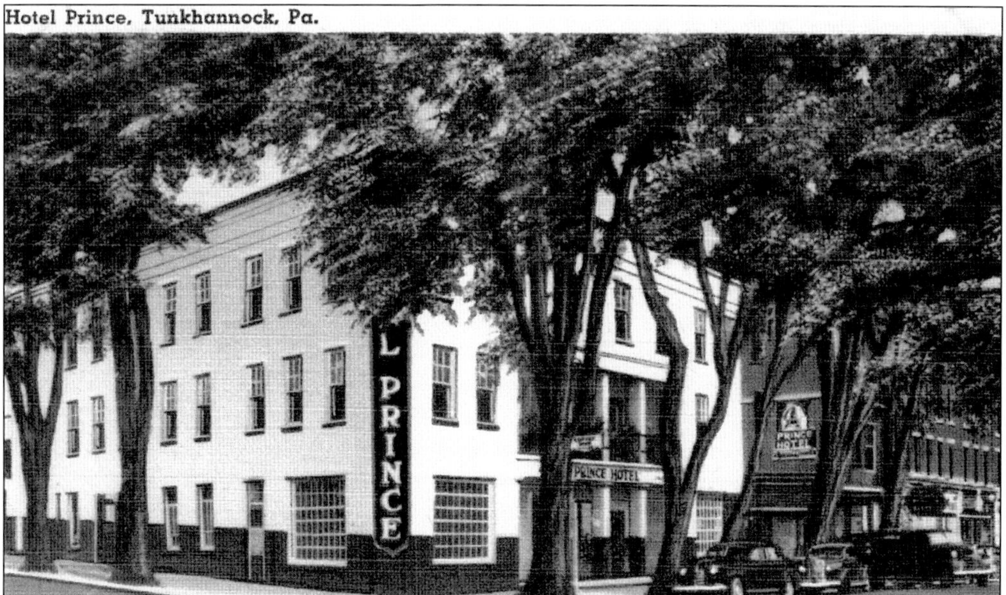

The Hotel Graham was sold to Dawson Howell and then to Mr. and Mrs. Bull. In 1944, Mr. and Mrs. Frank Prins bought the building and named it the Hotel Prins. In 1946, they sold the hotel to Hugh Westfall, and after that, it was known as the Prince Hotel.

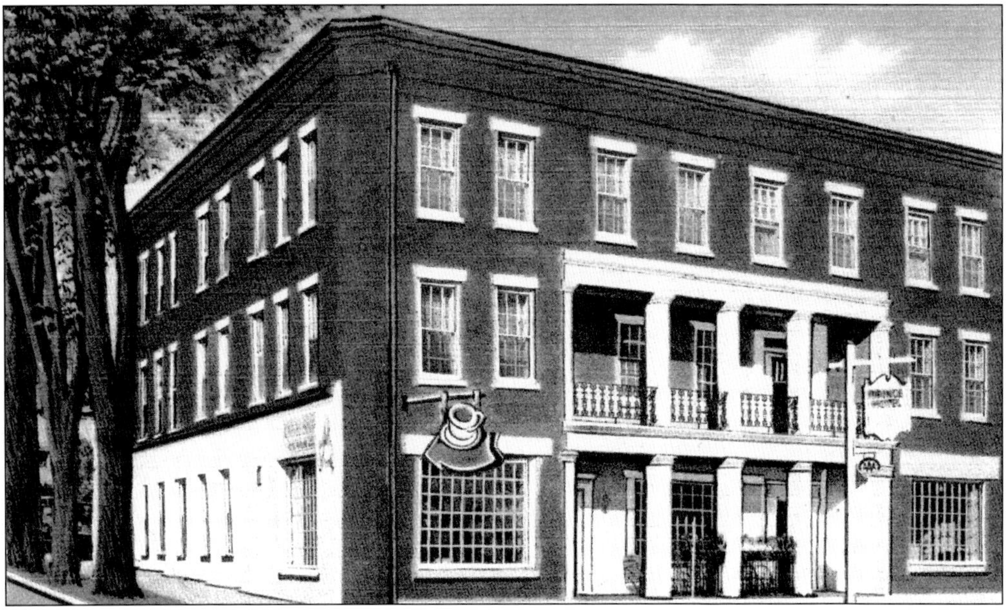

In 1956, Westfall sold the hotel to Kenneth Baker. Baker sold the hotel to William and Ruth VanDuzer in 1959. In 1966, James and Margaret Orasin bought the hotel from the VanDuzers, and in 1991, Milton and Lois Van Horn bought it from the Orasins.

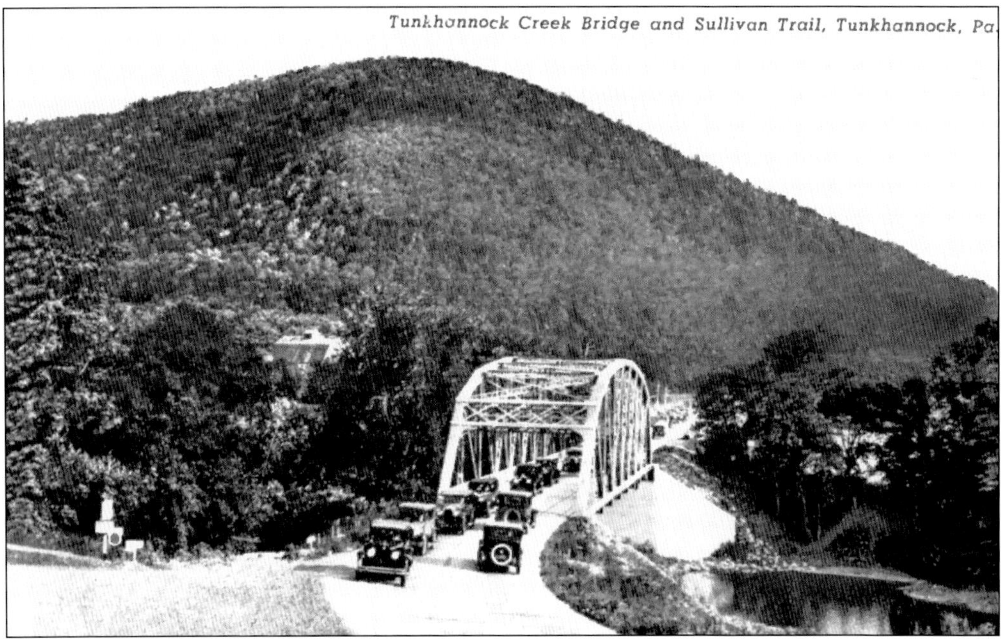

The bridge over the Tunkhannock Creek, on Route 92, was built in the 1920s. It was removed in 2000, and a new one was constructed when the Route 6 Tunkhannock Bypass was put in.

Citizen's National Bank, located on Warren Street in Tunkhannock, was founded in 1902.

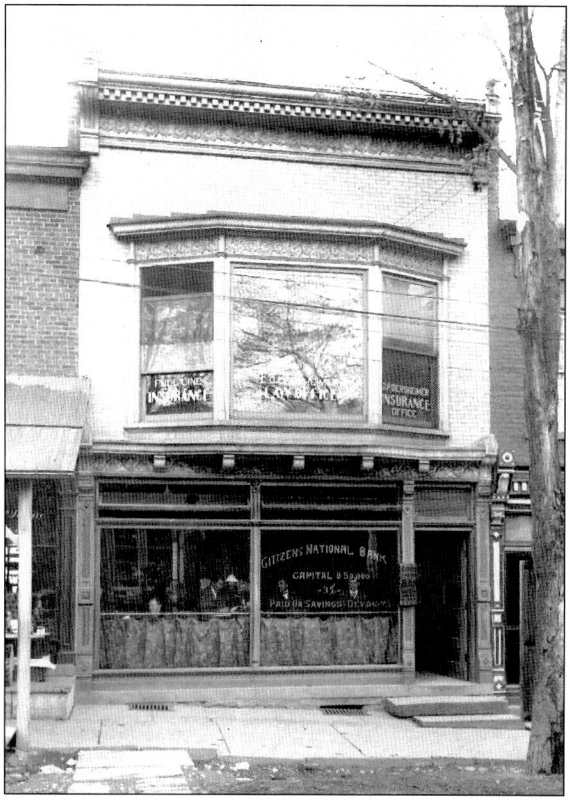

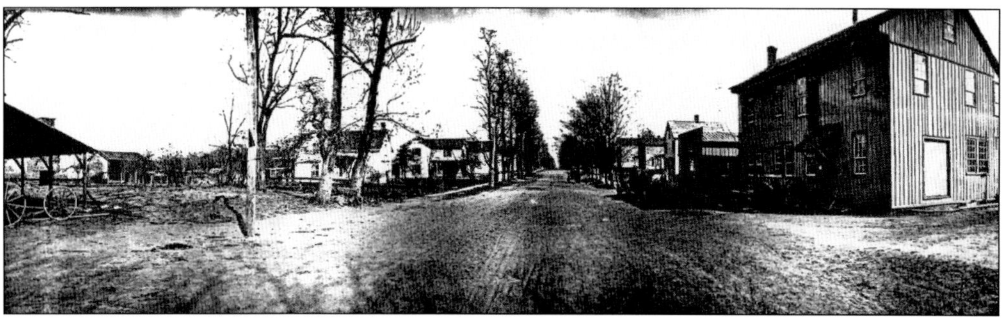

Maple Avenue in Tunkhannock, shown here at the intersection of West Tioga Street in 1902, was once known as Foundry Street because of the building on the right, the Avery and Miller Foundry. The building once housed a glass-cutting factory starting in 1895. In 1886, the glass company had a display at the Wyoming County Fair. William H. Winchester was the head of the cutting department. Homer Asheld, Robert Graham, and Dexter Stark are known to have worked at the factory. It was reported that in 1898, the glass factory closed and the proprietor, J. S. Edsall, moved to Pittston. The building was removed in 1940 to make way for a modern Sinclair gas station. The Sinclair station was removed in the 1980s, and a Texaco station stands there now.

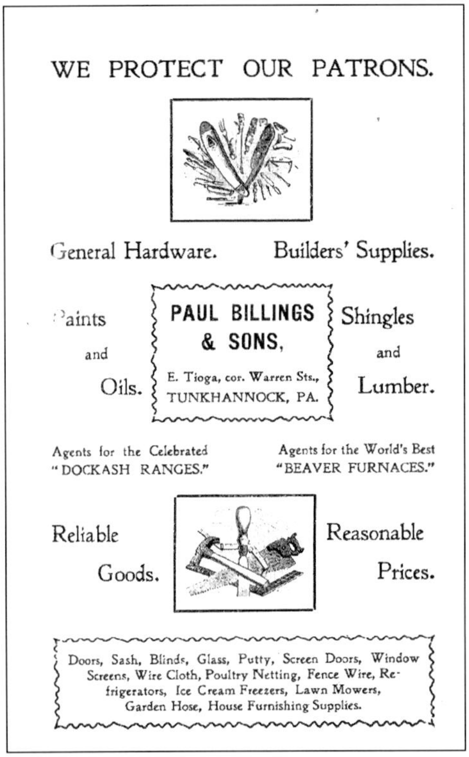

This advertisement for Paul Billings & Sons, located on the corner of East Tioga and Warren streets, is from the *1900 Hanford's Directory of Wyoming County.*

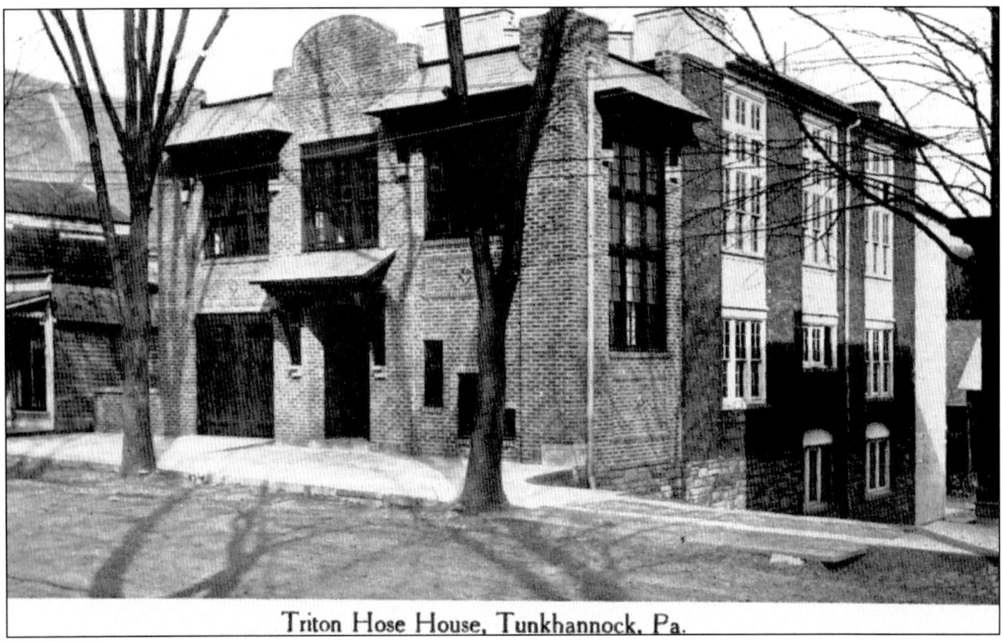

The Triton Hose Company was formed in 1872 after an 1870 fire started at the corner of Bridge and Tioga Streets and burned southward for three and a half hours. This building is the second firehouse, built in 1909 at a cost of $10,000. The first firehouse was built in 1890 and was later used as Tunkhannock Public Library. The library has since moved to a new building on Route 6 near the bottom of Mile Hill. This card is postmarked 1912.

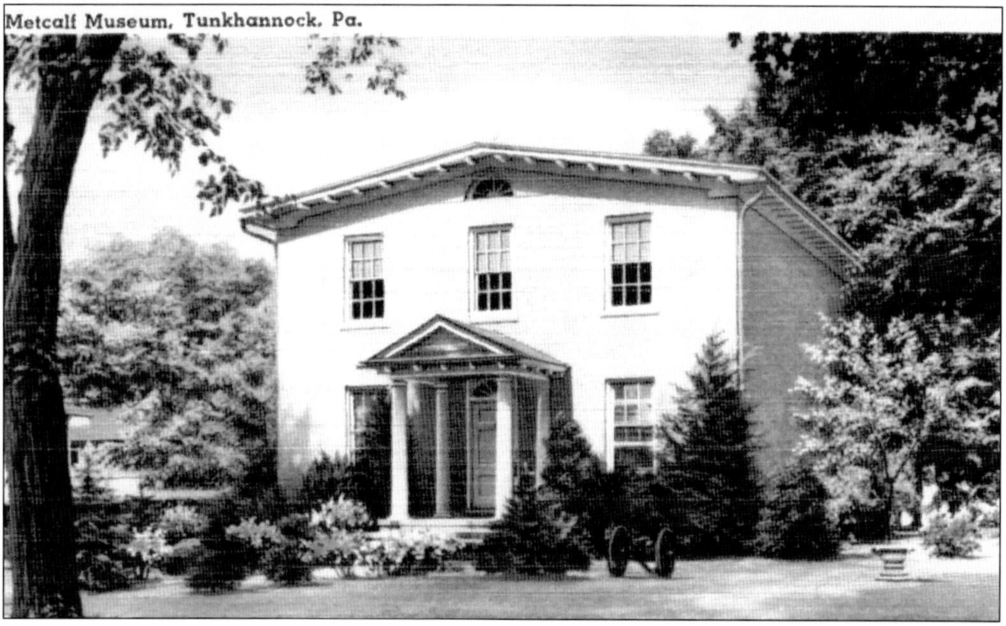

The Metcalf Museum was started in 1936 by H. P. Metcalf. It was located on Harrison Street and contained Metcalf's personal collection. H. P. and Mrs. Metcalf both died in 1946, and the museum was closed in 1950.

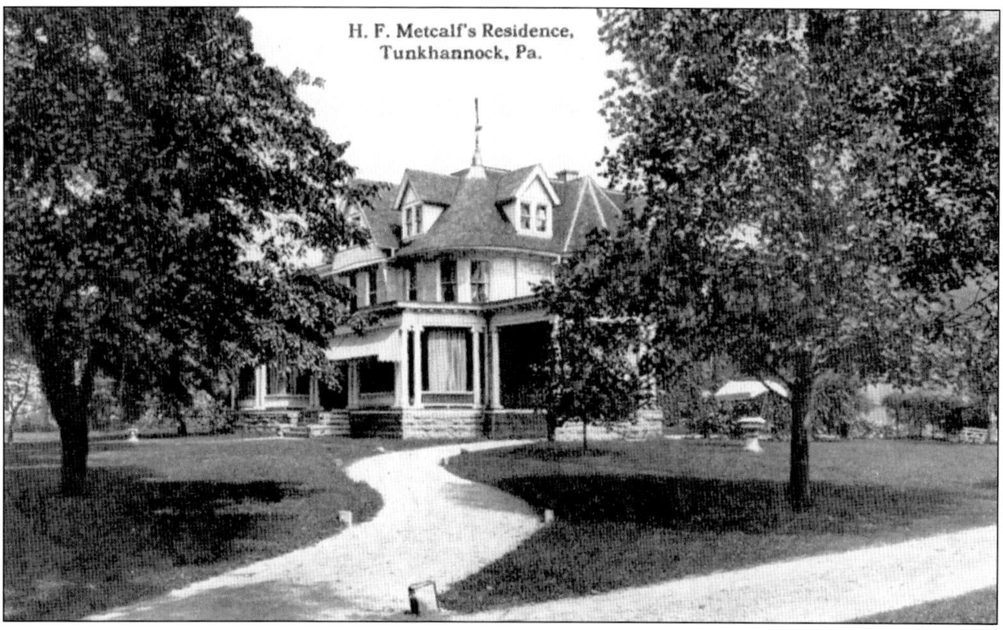

The residence of H. F. Metcalf is shown in this unused postcard.

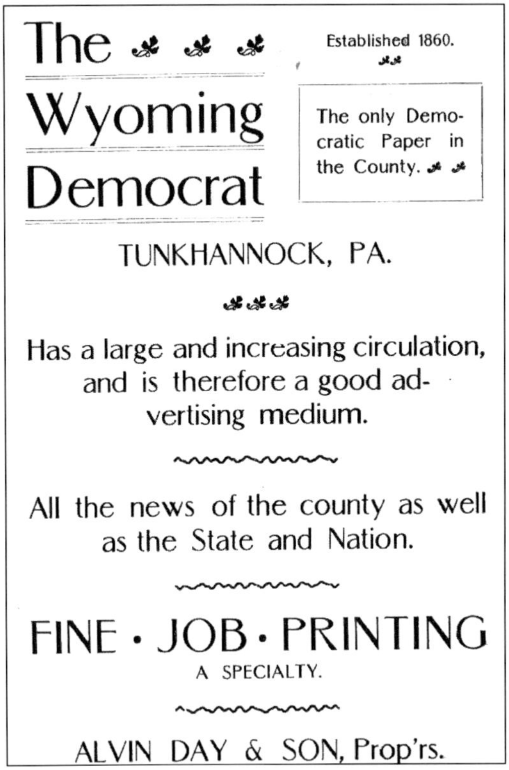

The *Wyoming County Democrat* was founded in 1854 as the *North Branch Democrat* after the North Branch Canal. The name was changed in 1867. This advertisement appears in the *1900 Hanford's Directory of Wyoming County.*

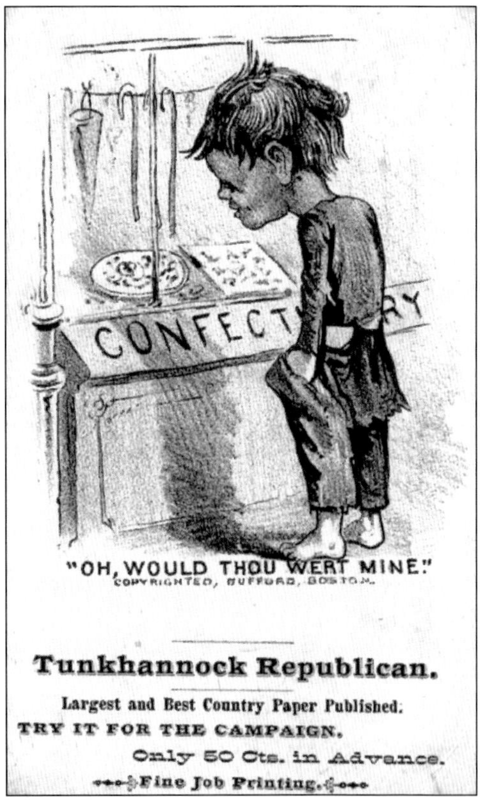

This card advertises the *Tunkhannock Republican,* which was in operation from 1869 to 1904.

Two

THE NORTHERN EDGE

Braintrim Township began in 1782 as one of the original Connecticut townships and is said to have gotten its name from Braintree, Connecticut. In 1790, Braintrim was one of the original townships when Luzerne County was formed. In 1842, it became part of Wyoming County.

Laceyville was incorporated on December 9, 1902, from Braintrim Township. Located on the northwest corner of Wyoming County on the North Branch on the Susquehanna River, the area was a campground for the Tuscarora Indians going to and from the Six Nations in New York State.

The first white settlers came to the area starting in 1766 from Connecticut and settled along the Tuscarora Creek by the Susquehanna River. The area was first known as Skinners Eddy before it became known as Braintrim. Its first post office was built in 1822.

In 1841, Laceyville was named after influential resident Henry W. Lacey, and the Laceyville post office was founded that same year.

The North Branch Canal was completed in 1857, and the railroad replaced the canal in the late 1860s. In 1893, the town's first newspaper, the *Braintrim Messenger,* was founded.

Lemon Township, named in honor of Associate Judge Percifer Lemon, was formed from Nicholson Township in 1847. The township was settled before 1800 by pioneers from Orange County, New York. Lake Carey, located in both Lemon and Tunkhannock Townships, is the second largest natural lake in Pennsylvania. Around 1800, the lake was named Barnum's Pond after Elijah Barnum, who owned a sawmill at the outlet of the pond. It then became known as Marcy's Pond. It was finally given the name Lake Carey after Earl H. Carey, a blind man who had title to the land under the lake. By 1875, the lake had become a summer resort.

Meshoppen Township was incorporated in 1854 from Braintrim and Washington Townships. The Meshoppen Creek attracted settlers to the area because of its ability to power mills. In 1775, Thomas Wigton built a home and a sawmill on the creek, and in 1795, Mason Alden built a gristmill. Other mills were soon to follow.

Meshoppen Borough was incorporated from Meshoppen Township in 1879. Black Walnut, located between Meshoppen and Laceyville, was originally named Black Walnut Bottom after the walnuts on the bottom the creek in the area.

Washington Township was formed from Braintrim and Tunkhannock Townships in 1832. The first settlement in the township was at Carney Flats, at the present site of the Proctor & Gamble paper plant. A post office was established at Carney Flats in 1871. Washington Township is also the location of the Vosburg Tunnel, built from 1883 to 1886 by the Lehigh Valley Railroad in order to cut five and a half miles off the trip around the Vosburg neck. Vosburg was settled and named after Abraham Vosburg. Its post office was started in 1870, with Isaac Vosburg serving as postmaster.

Keiserville was originally called Witchhazel because of the witch hazel shrubs growing in the area. The name Keiserville came from Michael Keyser of Philadelphia, who bought the mills and property along the creek. After 1866, the area became known as Vose because the post office was located in the Vose Mill building that Keyser owned. The name reverted back to Keiserville with the closing of the mill and post office.

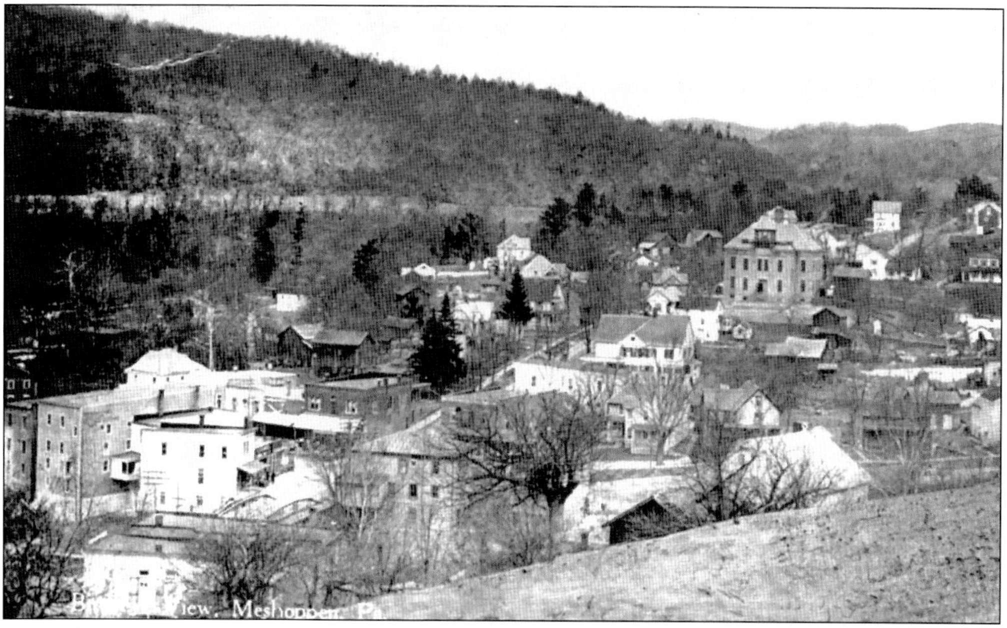

In this bird's-eye view of Meshoppen, the high school can be seen in the upper right corner. The bridge on Bridge Street can be seen in the lower left corner.

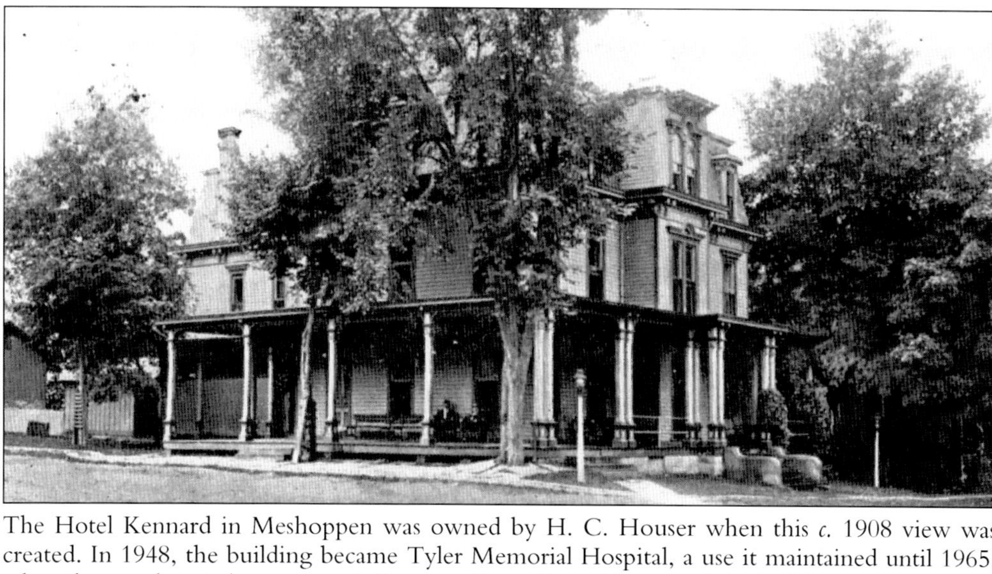

The Hotel Kennard in Meshoppen was owned by H. C. Houser when this *c.* 1908 view was created. In 1948, the building became Tyler Memorial Hospital, a use it maintained until 1965, when the new hospital was opened. Kenmar Home Furnishings used the building as a showroom after the new hospital was built. Kenmar has since built a new showroom, and the building is currently used as Kenmar's warehouse.

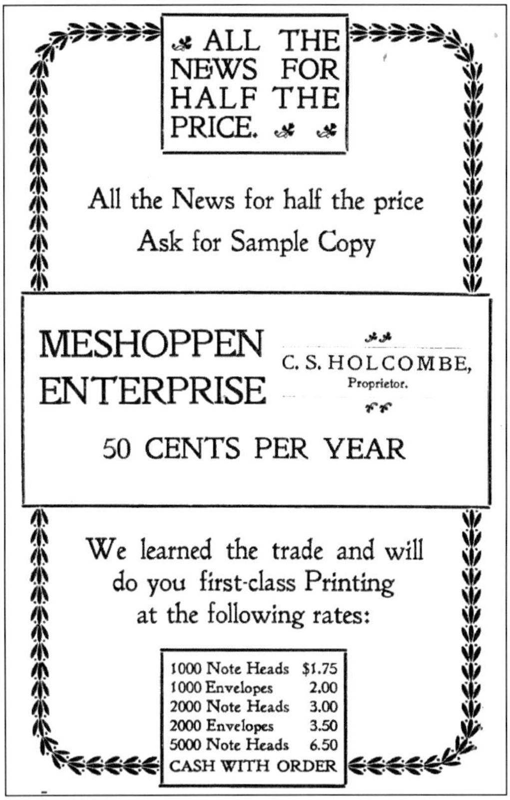

The *Meshoppen Enterprise,* advertised in the *1900 Hanford's Directory of Wyoming County,* was founded by C. S. Holcombe and later published by Kiah Mott and Roy Meyers. The paper ceased publication in 1943.

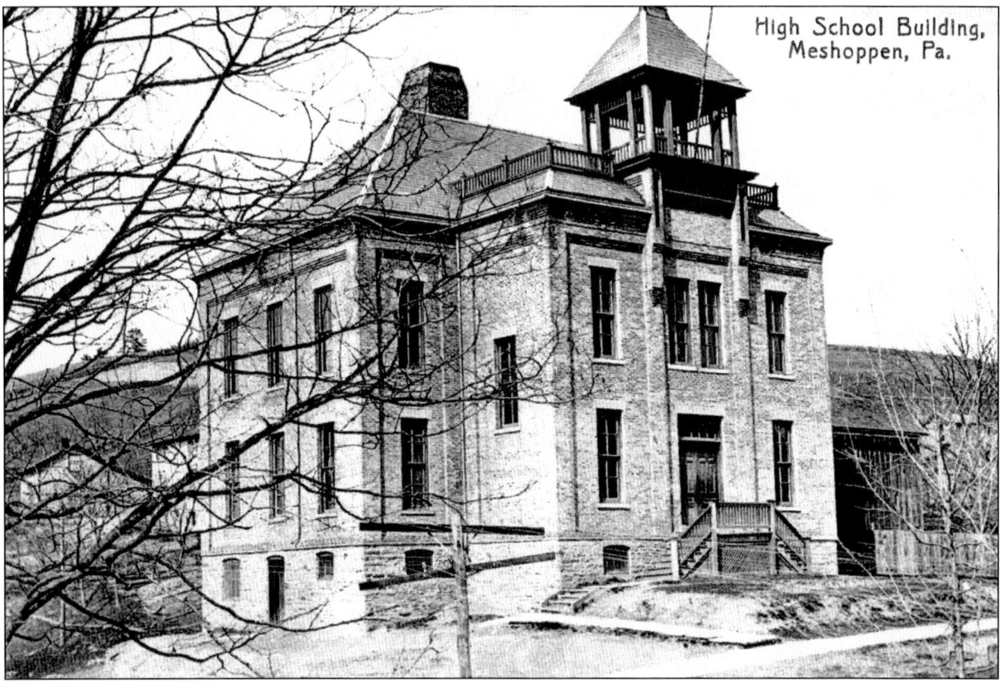

The Meshoppen High School, built in 1893, became a four-year high school in 1911. Frank Jarvis served as its principal. The building is no longer standing.

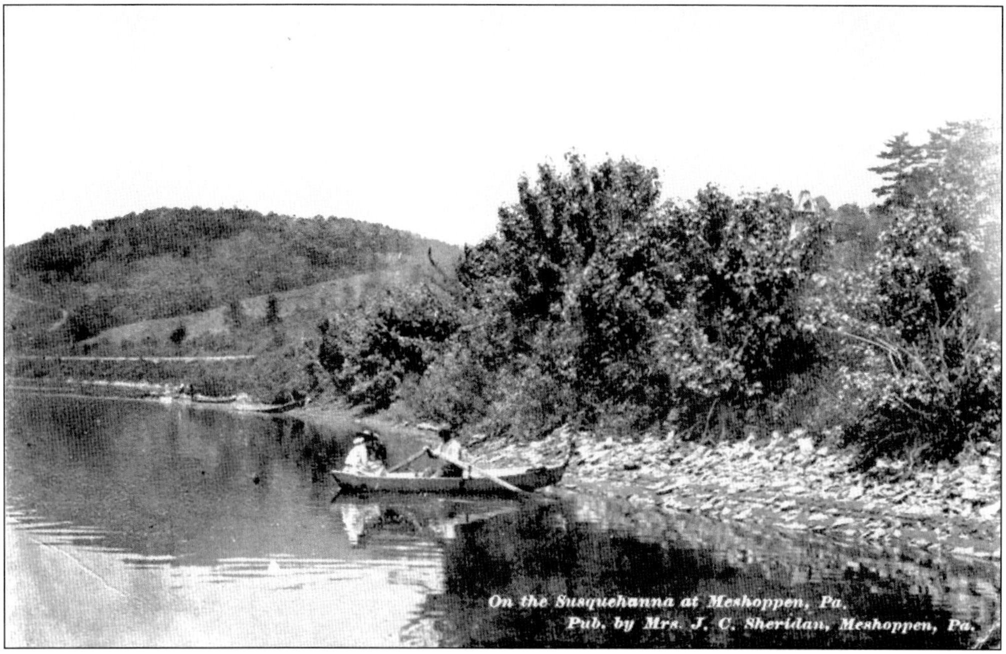

The Susquehanna River at Meshoppen, shown here *c.* 1908, is still used by boaters and fishermen.

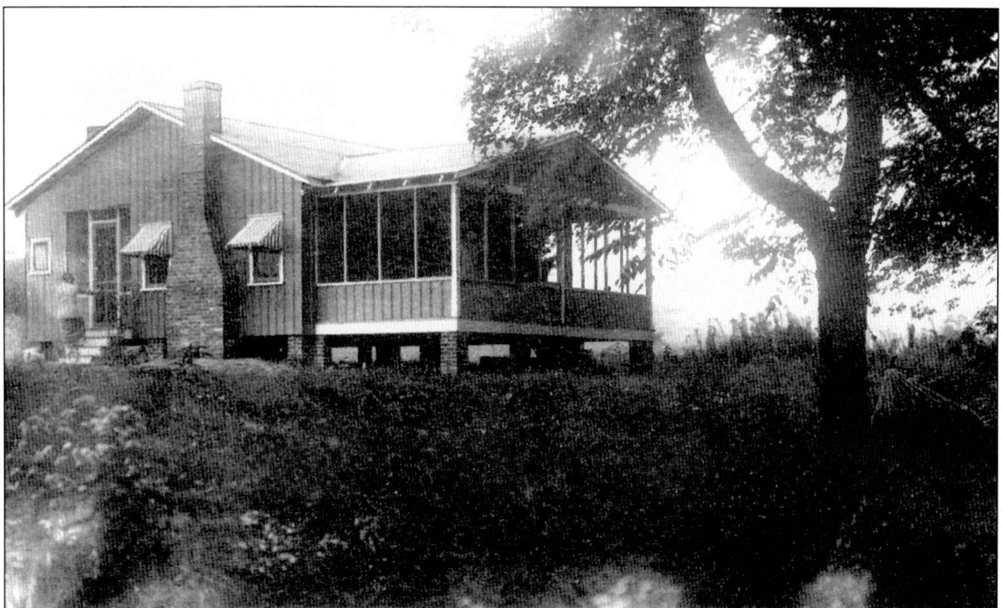

Myobeach, located up river from Meshoppen, was a popular area for summer cabins. Mrs. J. C. Sheridan, owner of the cottage shown here, published many postcards of Meshoppen.

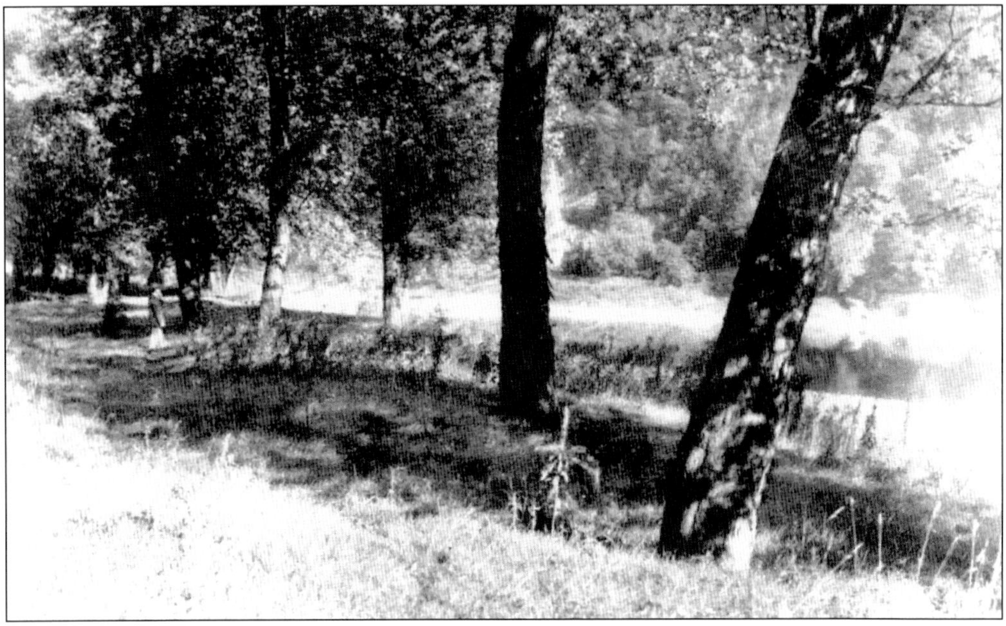

The Myobeach area near Meshoppen is still a beautiful spot on the river.

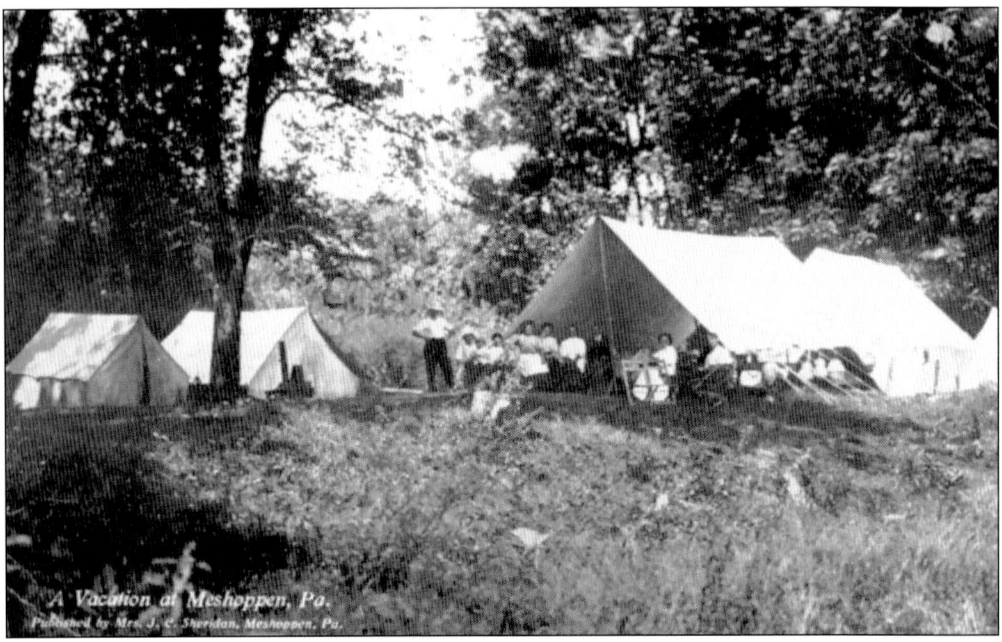

This card shows one of many nice riverside vacation spots in Meshoppen, a popular summer retreat for campers and fishermen.

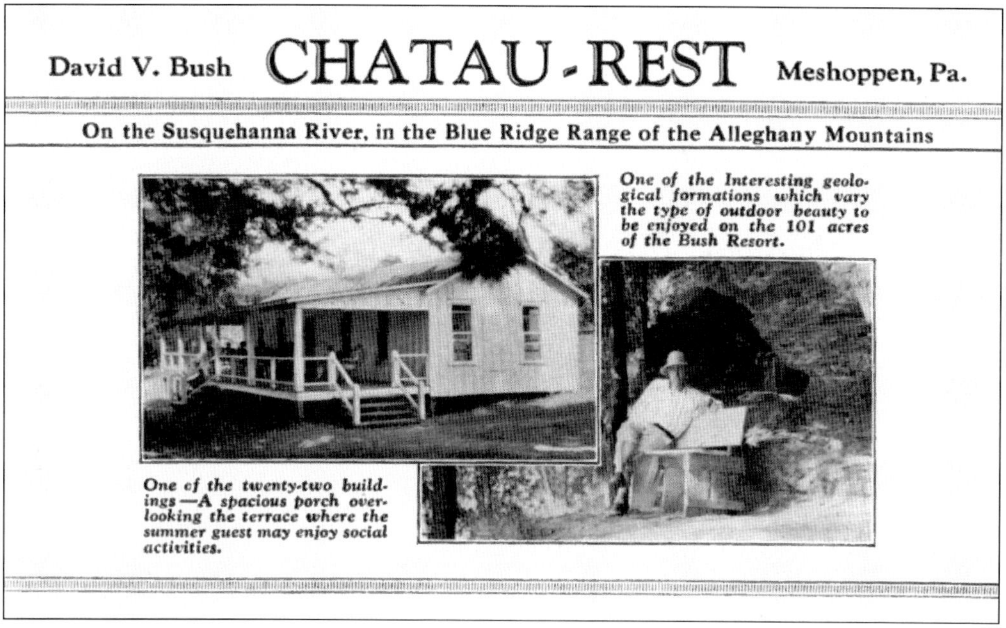

The Chatau Rest, owned by David V. Bush, boasted 101 acres overlooking the river. The resort contained 22 cottages.

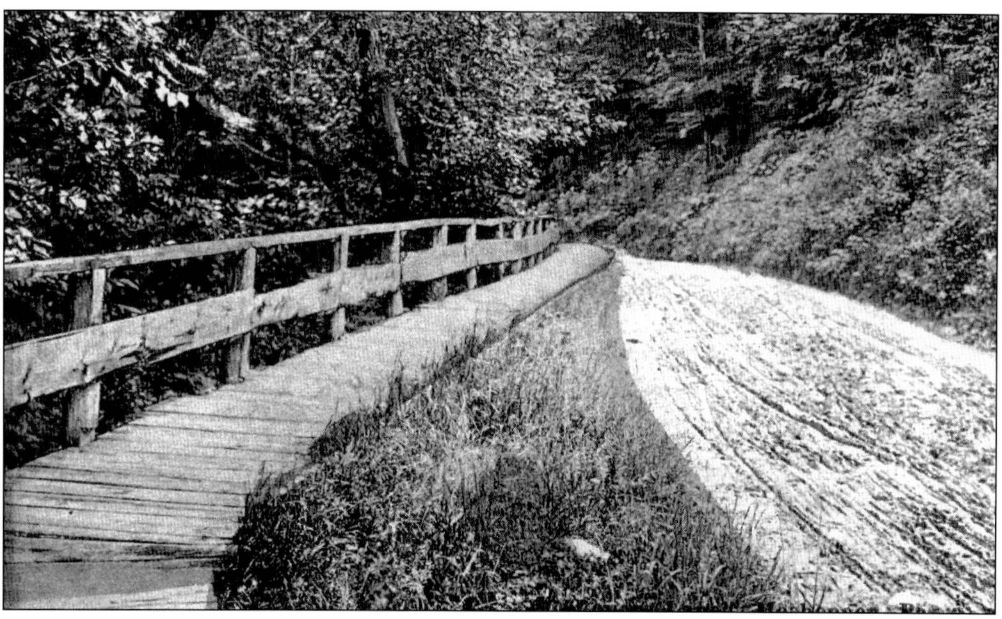

This unused postcard shows a dirt portion of Route 6 in Meshoppen. It connected Allen Street to the main part of town.

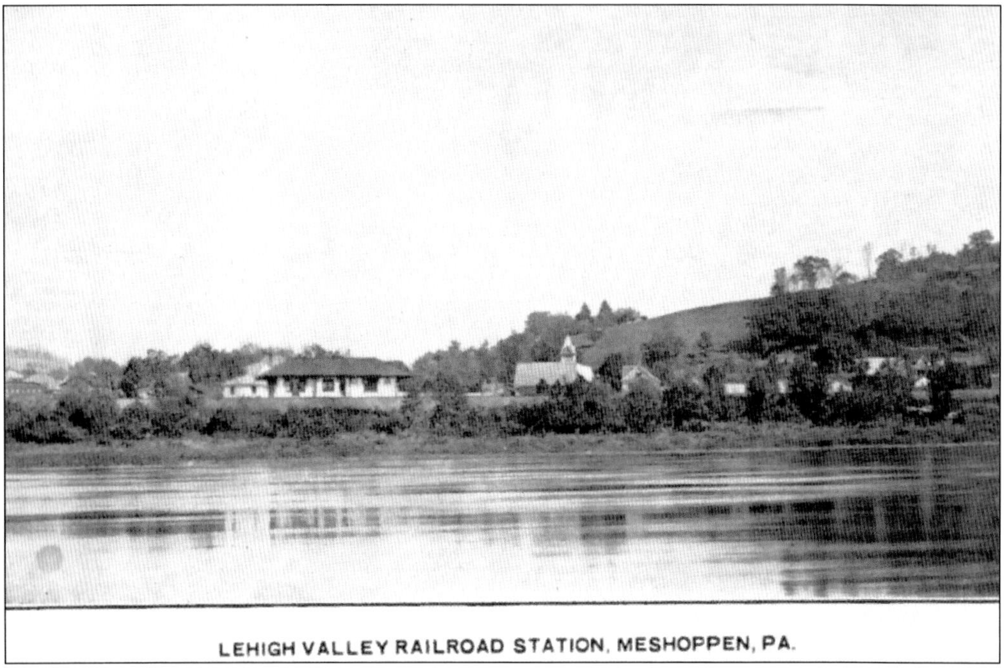

The Lehigh Valley Railroad station in Meshoppen was built in 1911 and was used until passenger service was stopped in 1930. The station still stands but is in need of repair.

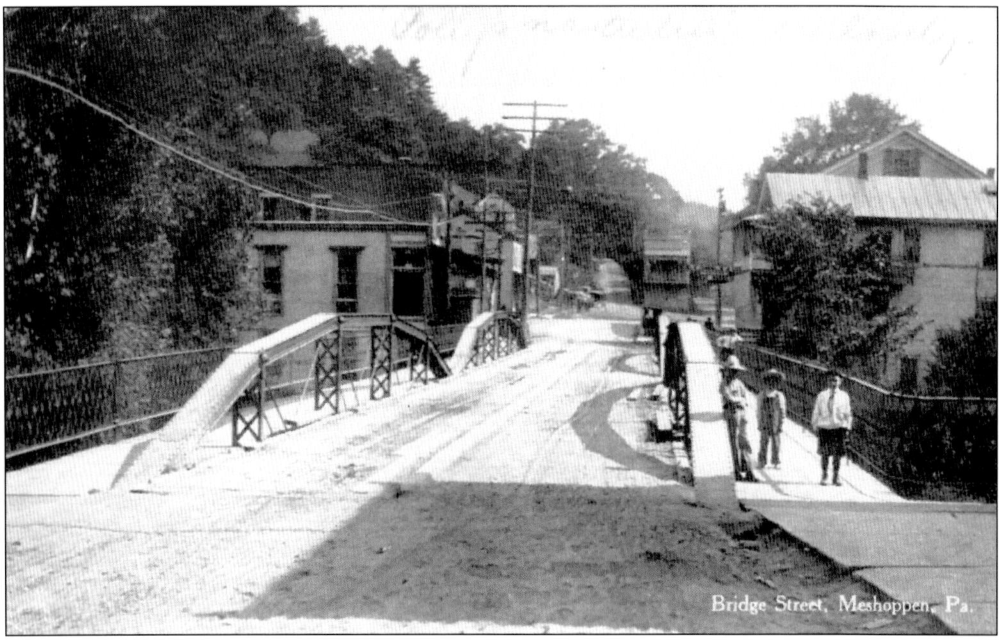

The bridge on Bridge Street in Meshoppen, shown in this view from 1909, has since been replaced.

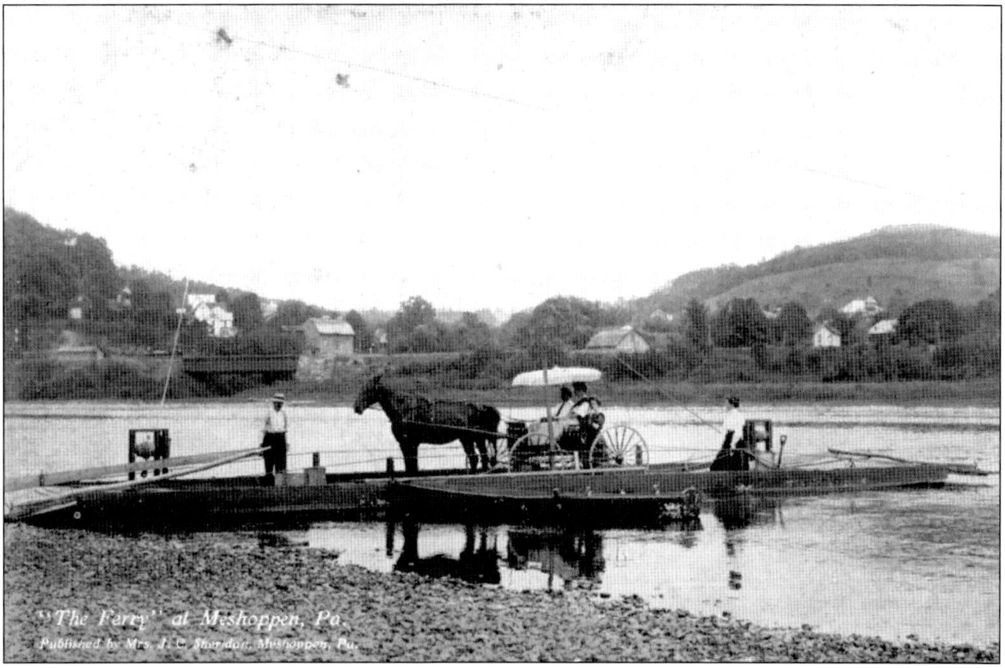

This ferry, owned by Orin Love, operated from Meshoppen to Pebble Beach on the opposite side of the river until 1930.

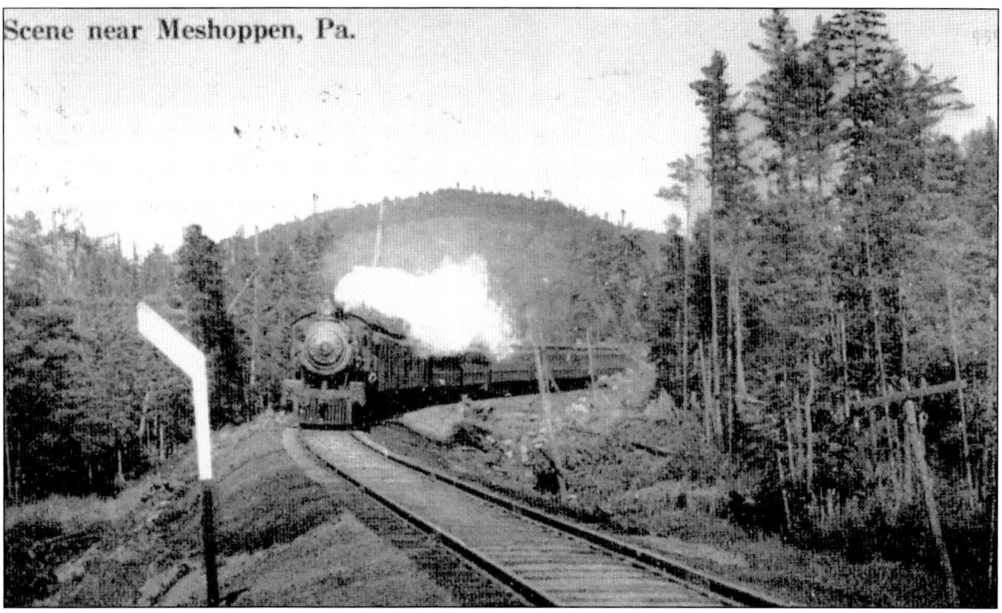

The Lehigh Valley Railroad ran next to the Susquehanna River through the entire county. This *c.* 1915 view shows a steam locomotive on the tracks near Meshoppen.

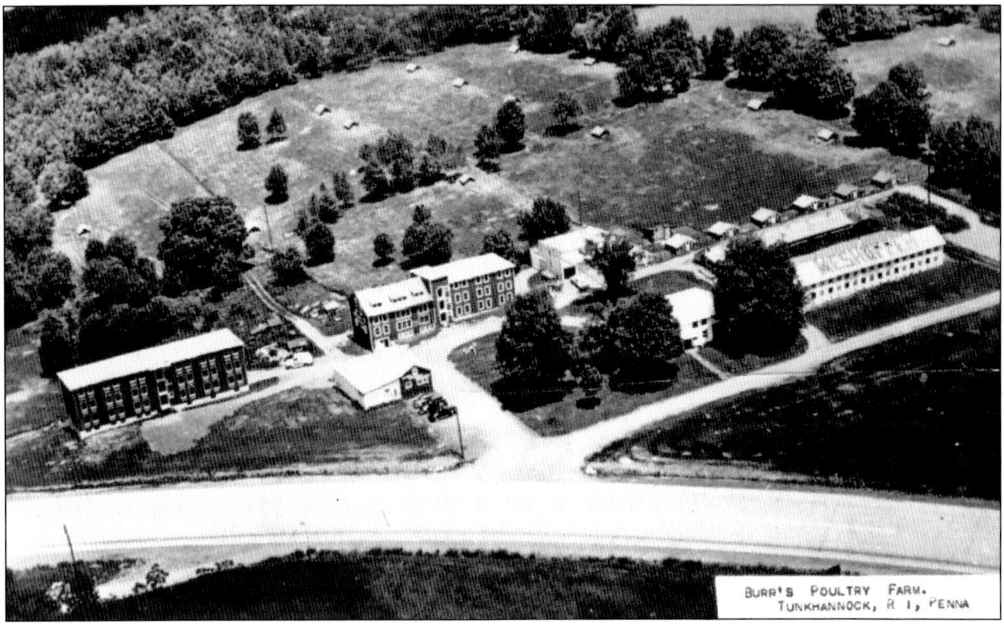

This aerial view of Burr's Poultry Farm, located at the intersection of Route 6 and Rail Road, dates from 1952. Although many of buildings in the photograph are still standing, they are in poor condition.

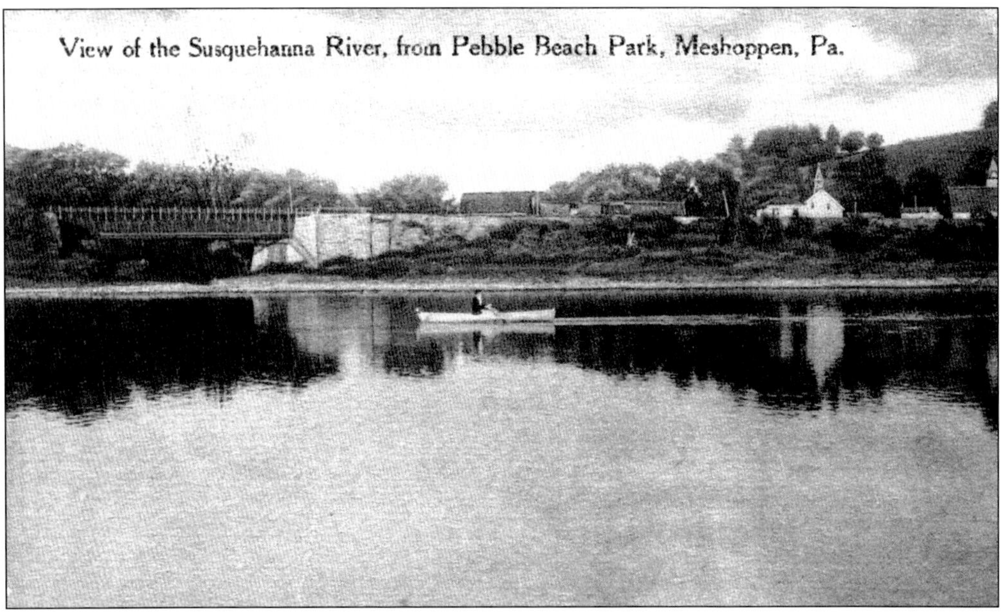

Pebble beach, shown here *c.* 1911, was a popular swimming and boating area across the river from Meshoppen.

The Methodist Episcopal church, located on Church Street in Meshoppen, was built in 1905 and looks much the same today.

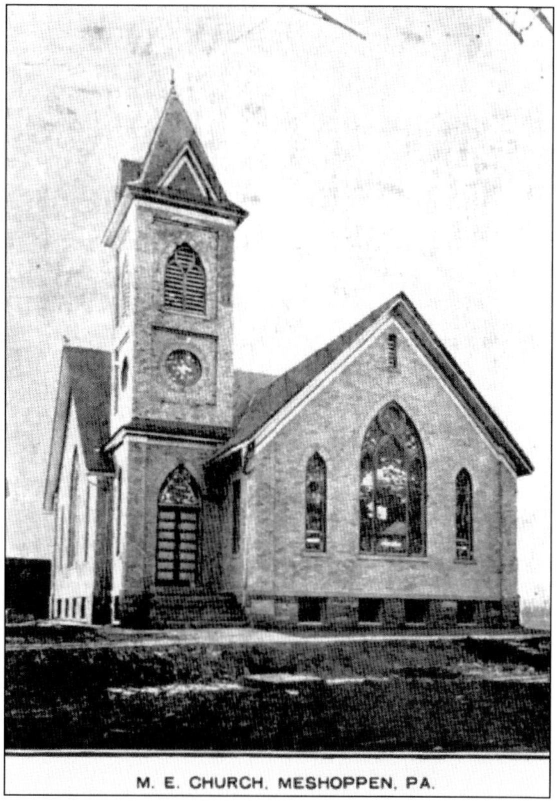

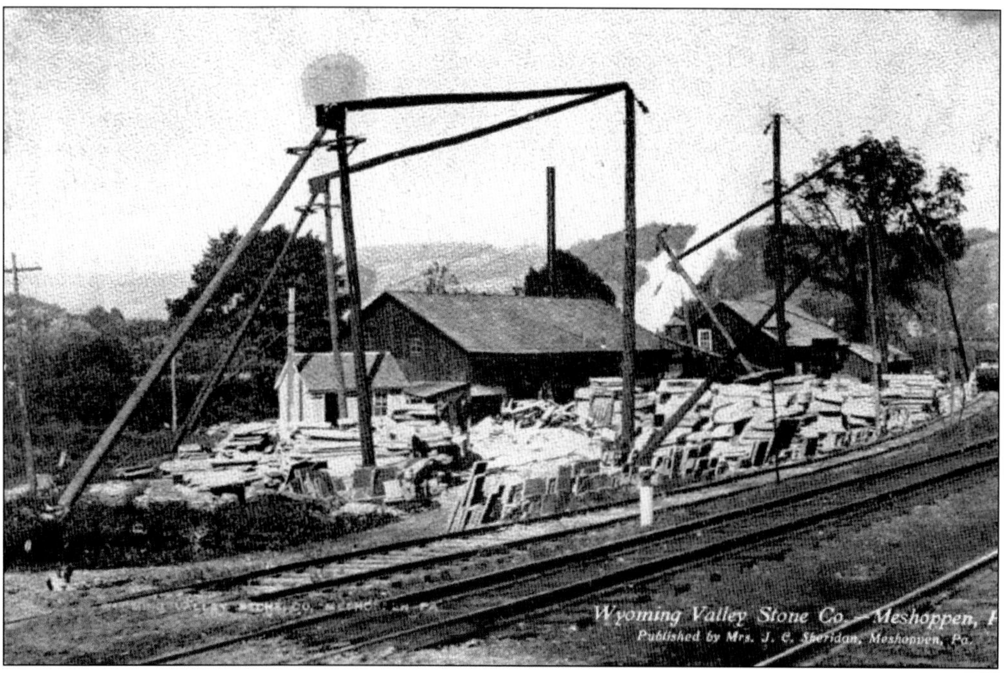

Mrs. Sheridan published this postcard view of the Wyoming Valley Stone Company of Meshoppen.

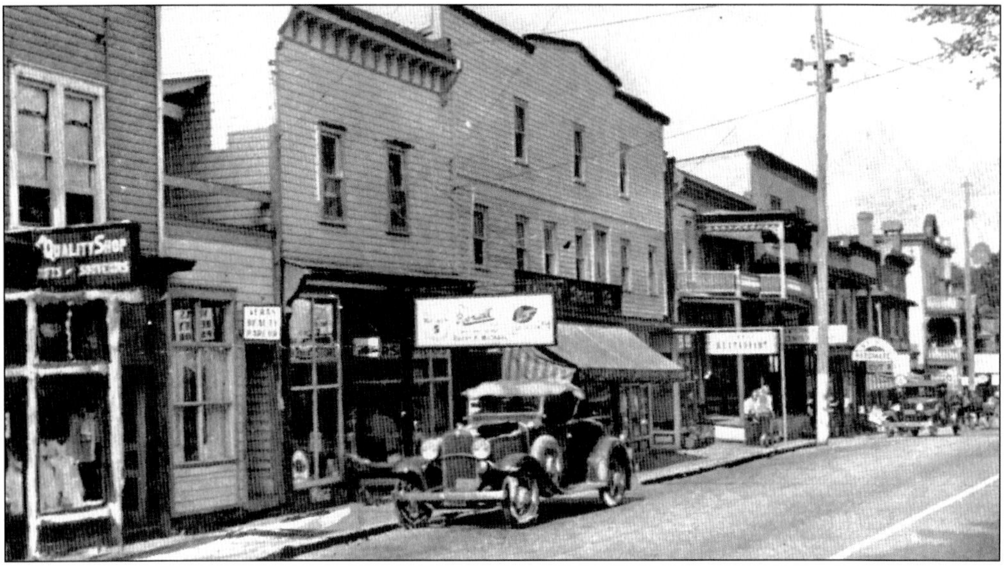

This view of Main Street in Laceyville includes some old cars.

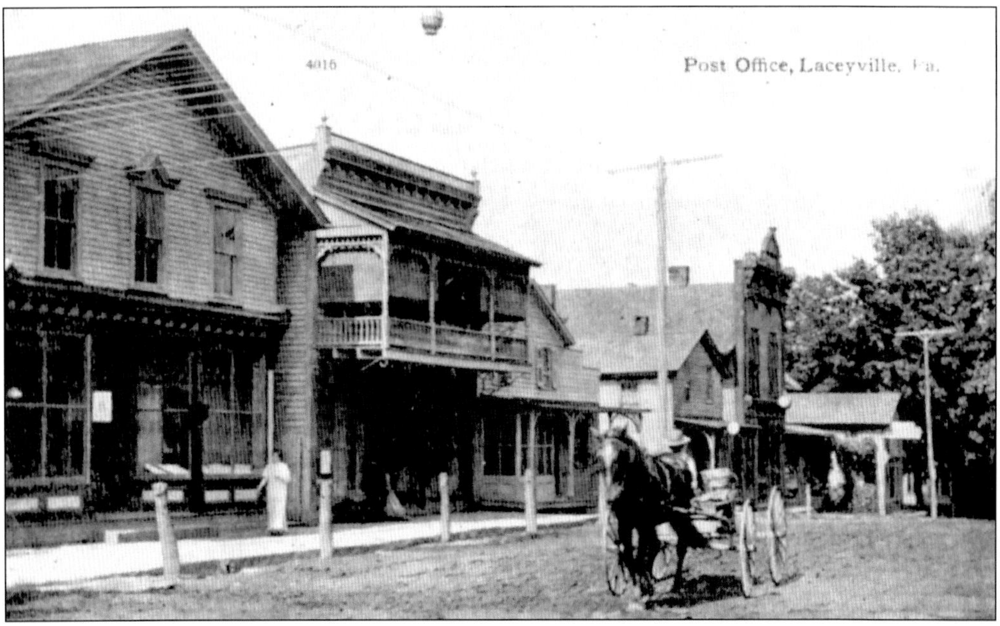

The post office in Laceyville dates back to 1841, when Thomas Parker was named postmaster. It is still located in the building shown here on Main Street.

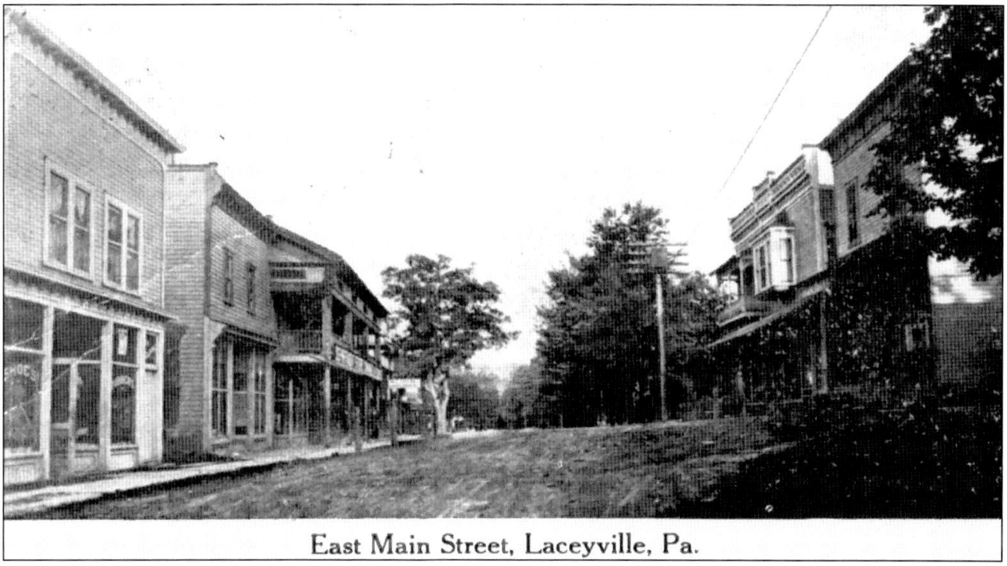

This is how East Main Street in Laceyville looked in 1912.

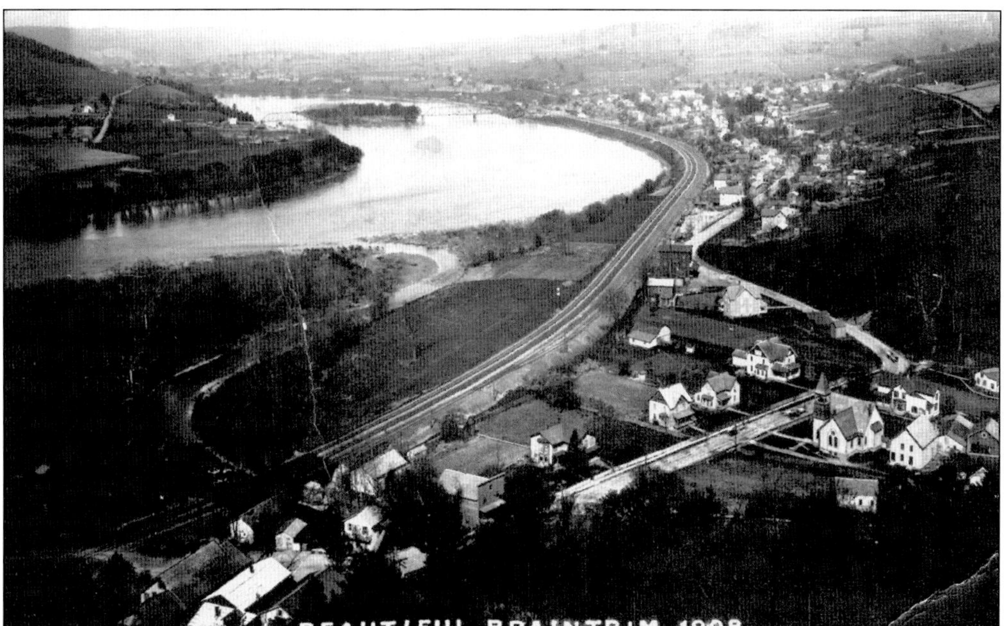

In this 1908 bird's-eye view of Braintrim, Skinners Eddy can be seen to the bottom right, and Laceyville is located at the top right.

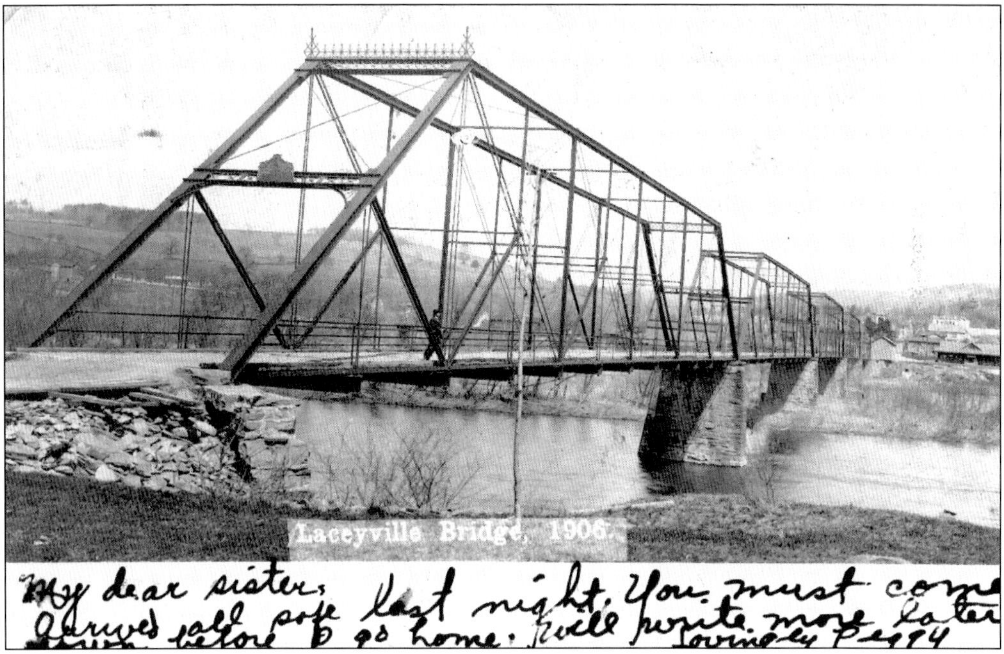

The first span across the Susquehanna River in Laceyville was a toll bridge built in 1899. This card shows the bridge in 1906, six years before the county purchased it and abolished the tolls. The bridge was damaged by Hurricane Agnes in 1972 and was replaced in 1974.

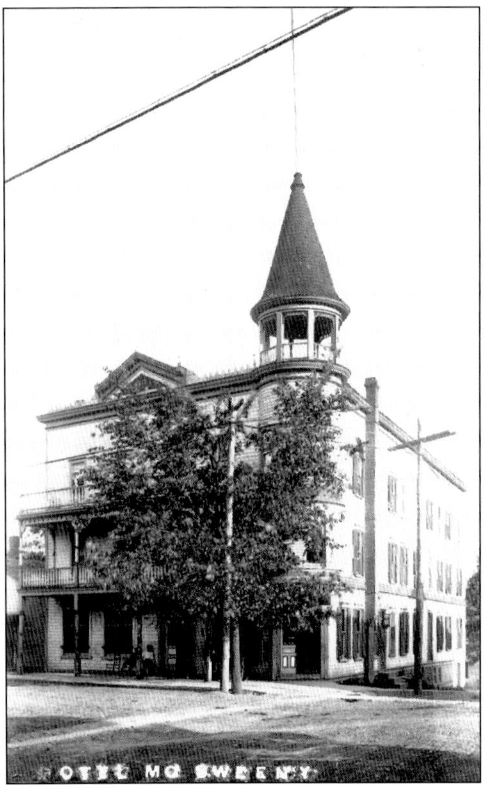

This card shows the Hotel Mingos in 1911, when it was known as the Hotel McSweeny. The hotel changed hands numerous times between 1892 and 1961. Other owners include David Michael, who bought it in 1915, and George Ciprich, who named it the John Sullivan Hotel.

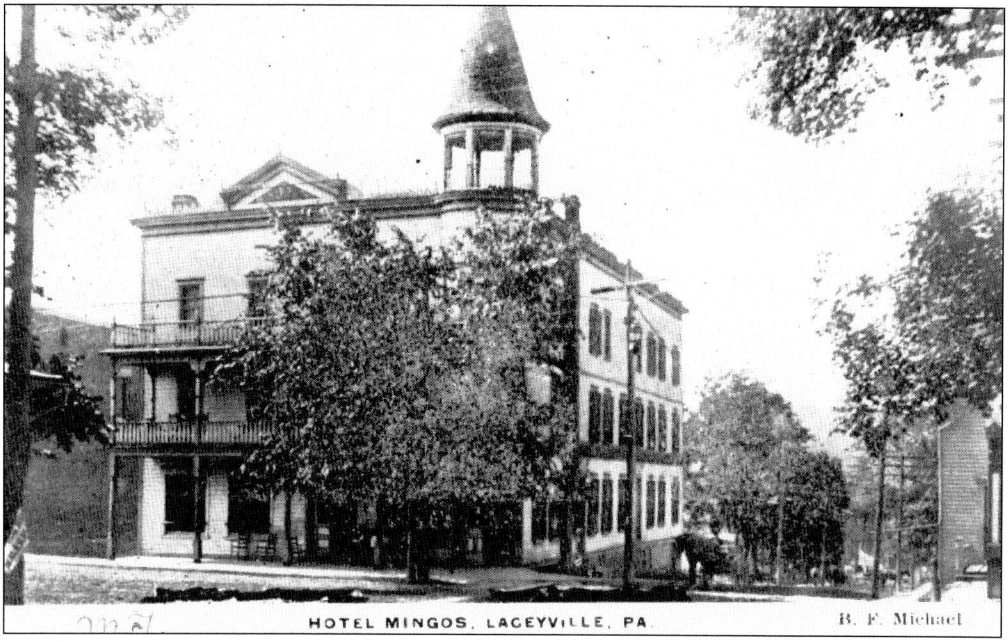

Hotel Mingos, located on the corner of Main and Church Streets in Laceyille, was built by Frank Mingos in 1892 and was destroyed by fire in 1961. This card also dates from 1911.

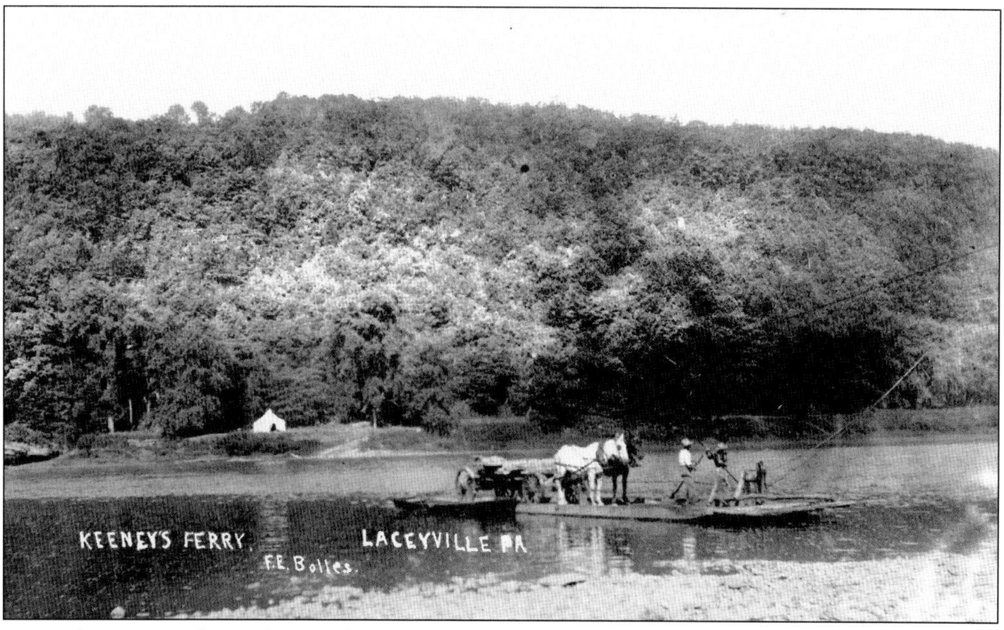

Keeney's Ferry was located in Rocky Forest, north of Laceyville, and was started by Thomas Keeney. The ferry was used to carry flagstone across the river and was in business until the 1930s.

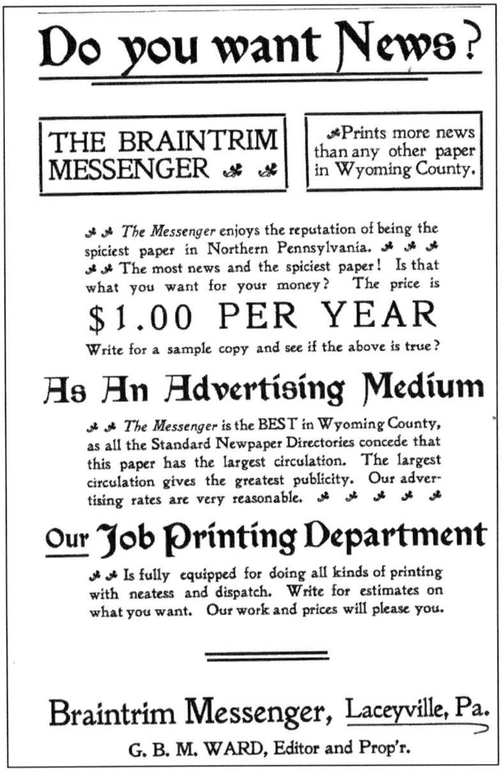

The *Braintrim Messenger*, advertised in the *1900 Hanford's Directory of Wyoming County*, was started in 1893. It changed its name to the *Laceyville Messenger* after the borough of Laceyville was formed. It remained in business until 1919.

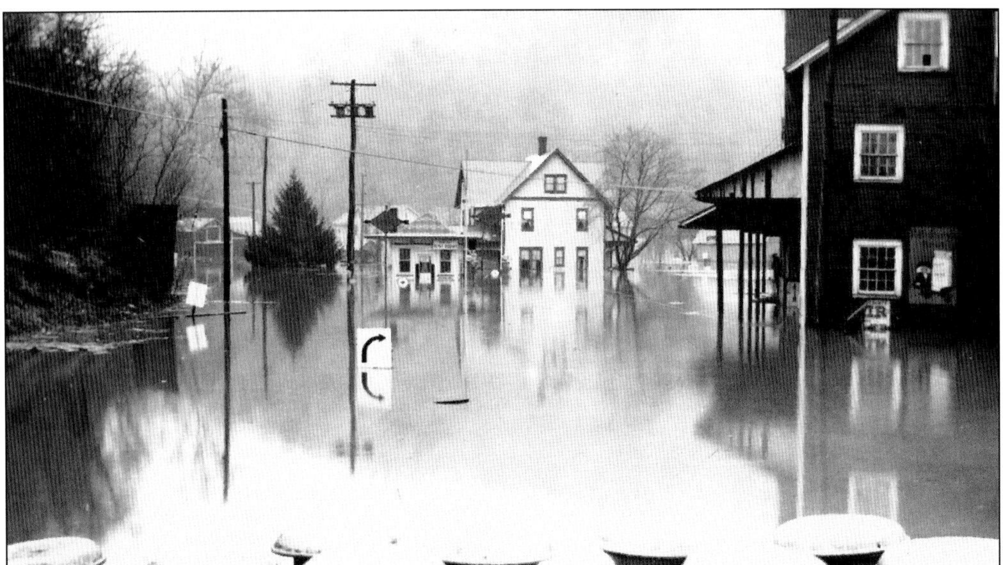

Skinner's Eddy was named after Ebenezer Skinner and his son Wait. The Skinners settled in the area in 1792, and Ebenezer died there in 1804. This view shows Skinner's Eddy during the flood of 1936.

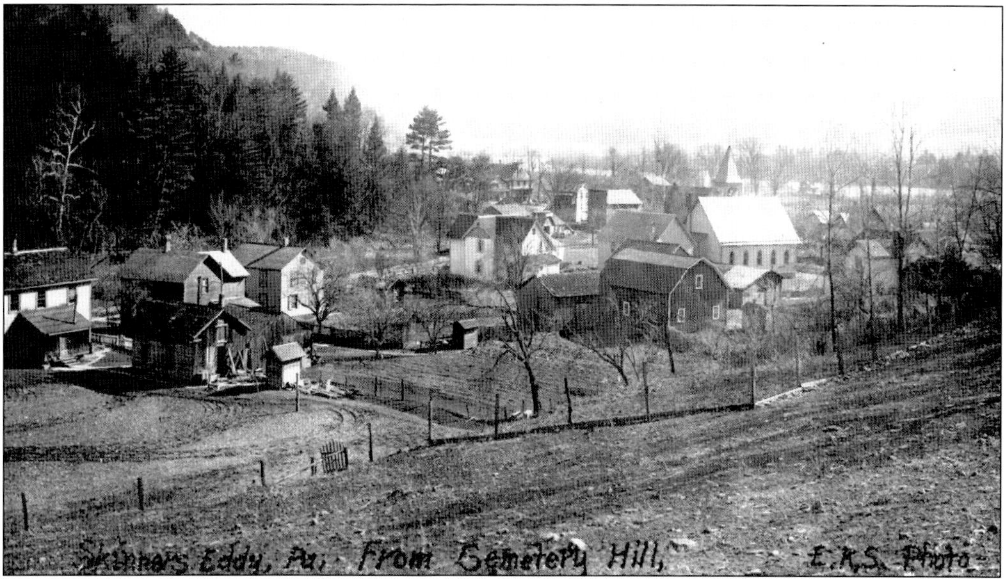

In this view of Skinner's Eddy from Cemetery Hill, the Methodist church steeple can be seen in the center of the photo postcard. Members built a new church after a flood damaged this building in 1975. The building still stands with a sign proclaiming it as the Church Mall.

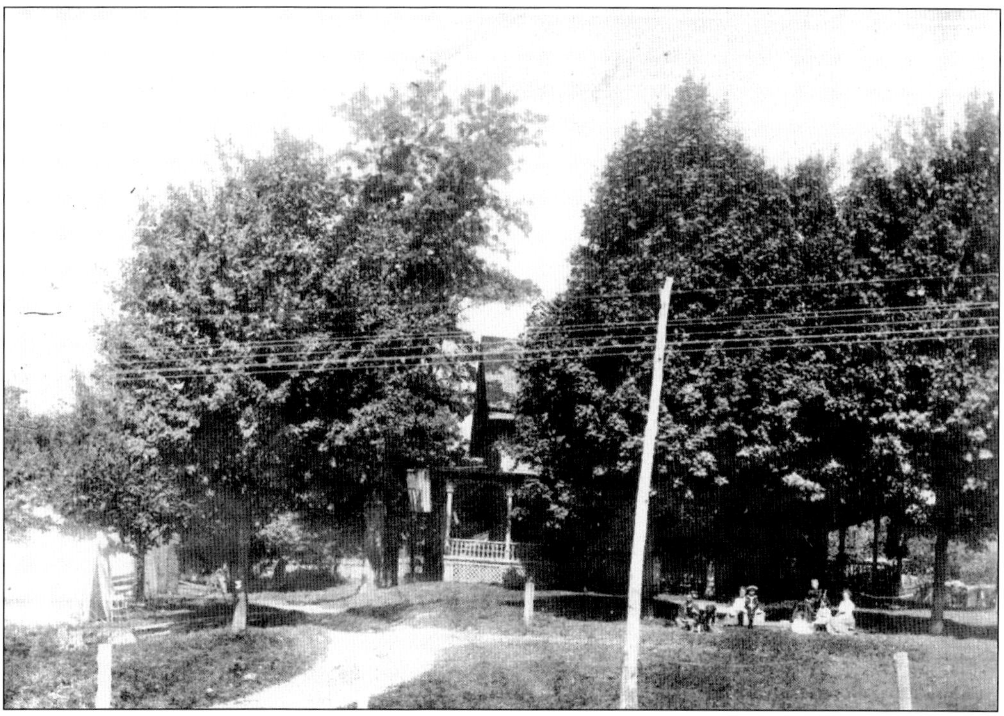

This building in Black Walnut, located between Meshoppen and Laceyville, is believed to have become the current home of the American Legion Post 510, Rought Hall.

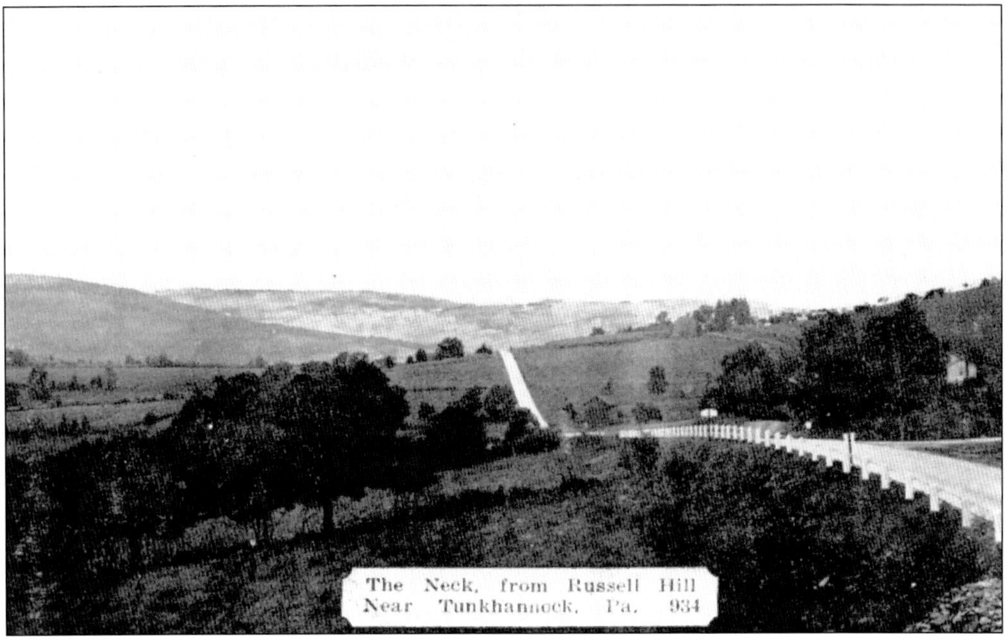

This view of Russell Hill includes Route 6.

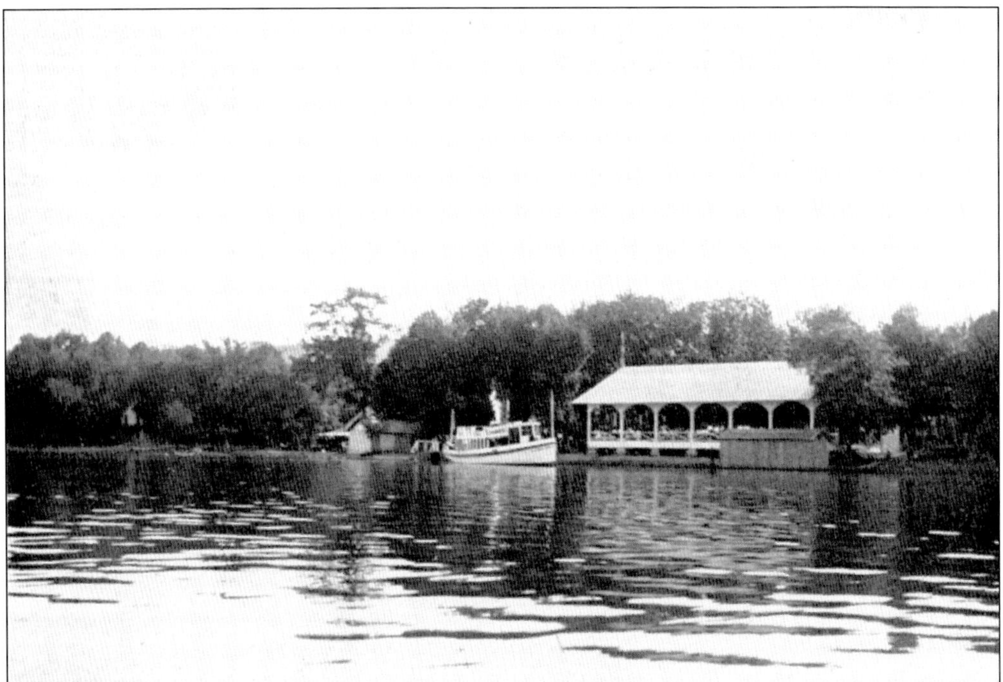

Lake Carey at one time had three steamboats plying its waters—the *Empress of the Lake,* owned by Asa Stevens; the *Lilly of the Lake,* owned by Ed Stevens; and the *Rosalind,* owned by John Redington. The *Rosalind* was brought in from Harvey's Lake in Luzerne County. This photograph shows either the *Rosalind* or the *Lilly of the Lake.*

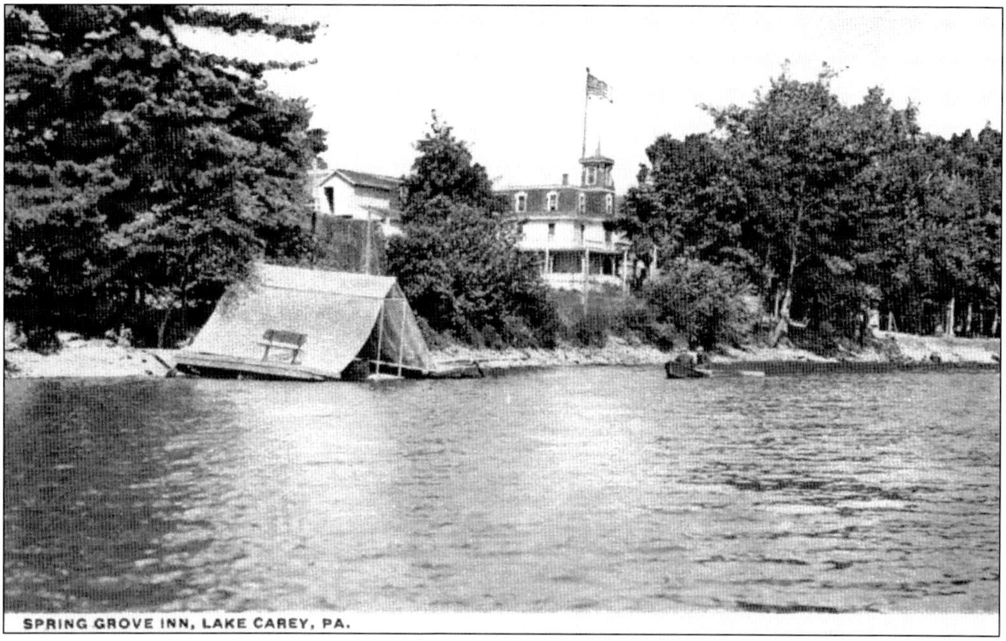

The Spring Grove Inn at Lake Carey was named for the fresh spring water that was found in the grove where it was located. The inn was built in 1887. It was purchased in the 1960s by the Knights of Columbus, who renamed it the Nite's Inn. It was then purchased by a Dr. Lopatofsky, and in 1983, it was destroyed by fire.

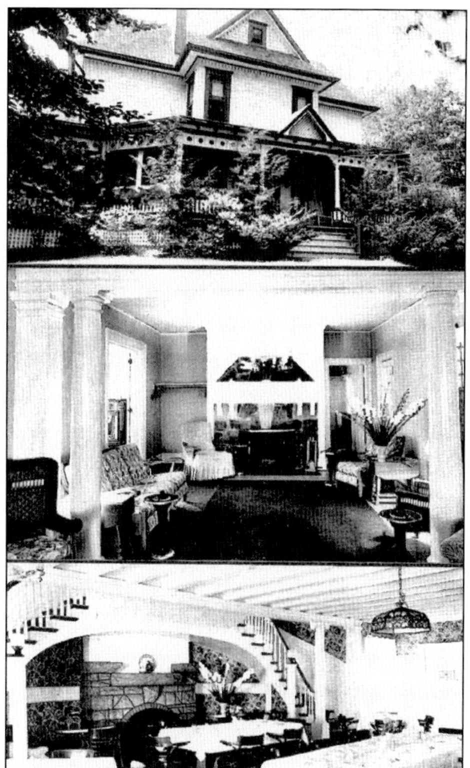

The Lakewood Club was started in the 1930s by Mr. and Mrs. Nat Stevens Sr. The club was located on Mud Pond, also known as Stevens Lake, in a three-story summer home the Stevens purchased from Judge Frank Wheaton. The club closed in 1947, and the building was converted into apartments before being destroyed by fire in 1971.

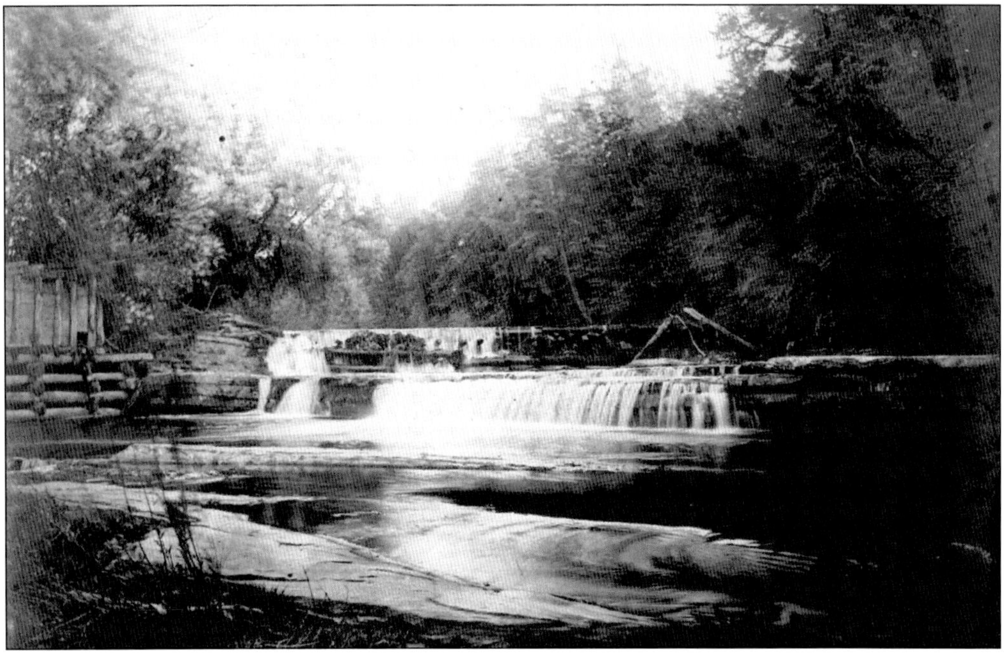

This card, postmarked 1907, shows the dam at Vose on the Meshoppen Creek. After 1866, the area of Keiserville became known as Vose because the post office was located in the Vose Mill. It eventually took the name of Keiserville again after the Vose post office closed.

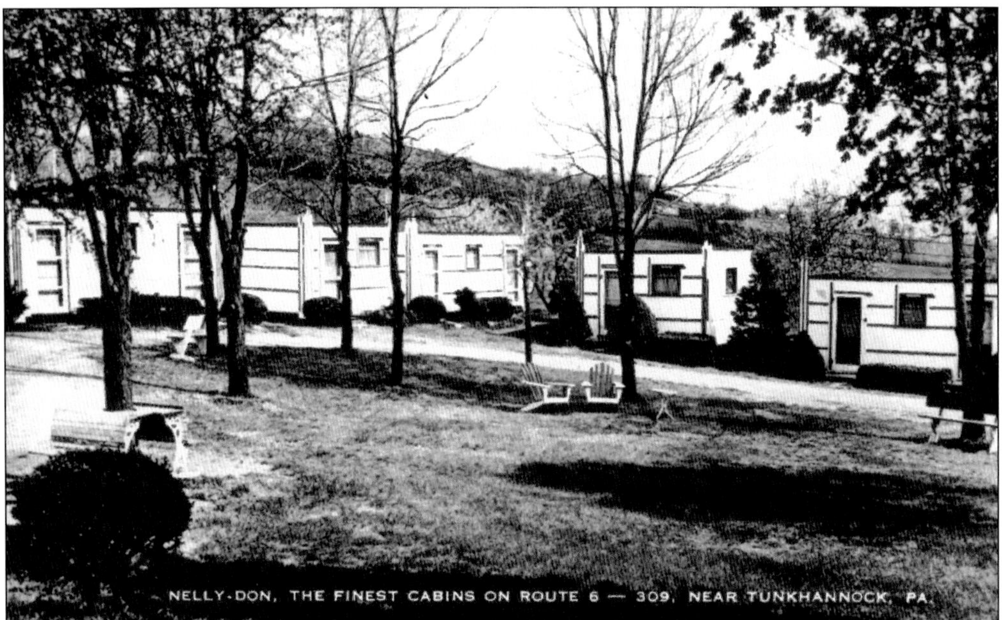

The Nelly-Don Cabins were named for Don and Nellie Robinson, who operated them for tourists. The Robinsons also operated a store that was located in front of the cabins near the intersection of Routes 6 and 87 on Russell Hill. A Texaco station is located there today.

Three

West of the River

Eaton Township was named for the hero of Tripoli, General Eaton. The township was created from a portion of the original Tunkhannock Township in 1817. In 1880, there were two post offices in the township—one at Eatonville and one in South Eaton. Post offices were later added in Thurston Hollow in 1890, and in Rosengrant and Lucasville (Sugar Hollow) in 1893.

Forkston Township was formed from Windham Township in 1844. It is named after the fork in the Mehoopany Creek near the town of Forkston. At one time, the town of Ricketts was located at the very southern edge of the township. Ricketts was formed as a lumber town with much of the lumber being hauled by railroad down through Noxen. The lumber industry also supplied hemlock bark to the Noxen Tannery.

Mehoopany Township was formed in 1844 from Windham Township. The name comes from the American Indian word *hoppeny,* which means "place of wild potatoes." At one time, the village was split into Mehoopany and North Mehoopany, with each town having its own post office. The North Mehoopany post office was established in 1889 with Joseph G. Burgess as postmaster, and it closed in 1964. Mehoopany's post office opened in 1840 with William H. Barnes as postmaster.

Monroe Township, named for Pres. James Monroe, was taken from Northmoreland Township in 1832. The towns of Beaumont and Evans Falls are located in Monroe Township.

North Branch Township was formed out of Forkston Township in 1857 and is named after the North Branch of the Mehoopany Creek, which flows through it. The first settlers were Winslow, Vose, and Lovelton. Azariah Winslow settled in the area of Lovelton *c.* 1800.

Northmoreland Township was one of the original townships set off from Luzerne County when Wyoming County was formed in 1842. The first post office in the township was opened in 1812, and Asa Keeler was the postmaster until his death in 1867. The township includes the town of Vernon, which once contained two churches, two stores, a feed mill, a dance hall, and a school. Only one church remains today. Vernon and Center Moreland each had its own post office at one time.

Noxen Township was incorporated in 1895 from Monroe Township. The name was chosen by the Post Office Department (now the U.S. Postal Service). The town was laid out by a farmer named Ziba Sickler to include 200 lots with a 160- by 400-foot central park.

Windham Township was settled by people from Windham County, Connecticut, who named the township after their old home. The towns of Golden Hill, Jenningsville, North Flat, and Scottsville, all located in the township, each had a post office. Golden Hill's post office was established *c.* 1845, Jenningsville's was established in 1855, North Flat's was established *c.* 1838, and Scottsville's was established in 1826.

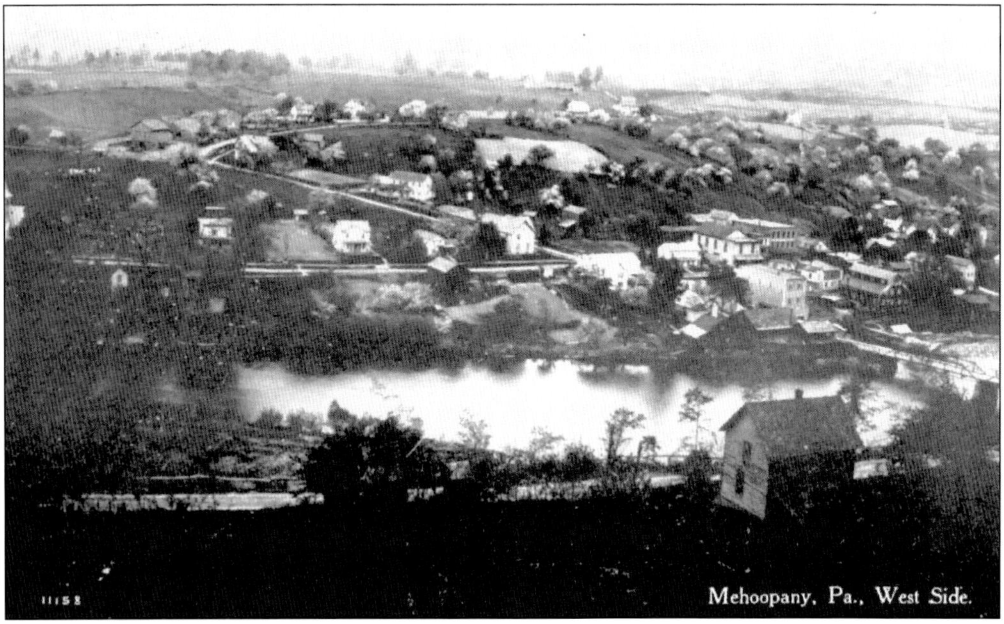

The bridge over the Mehoopany Creek can be seen this photograph, showing Mehoopany from across the creek.

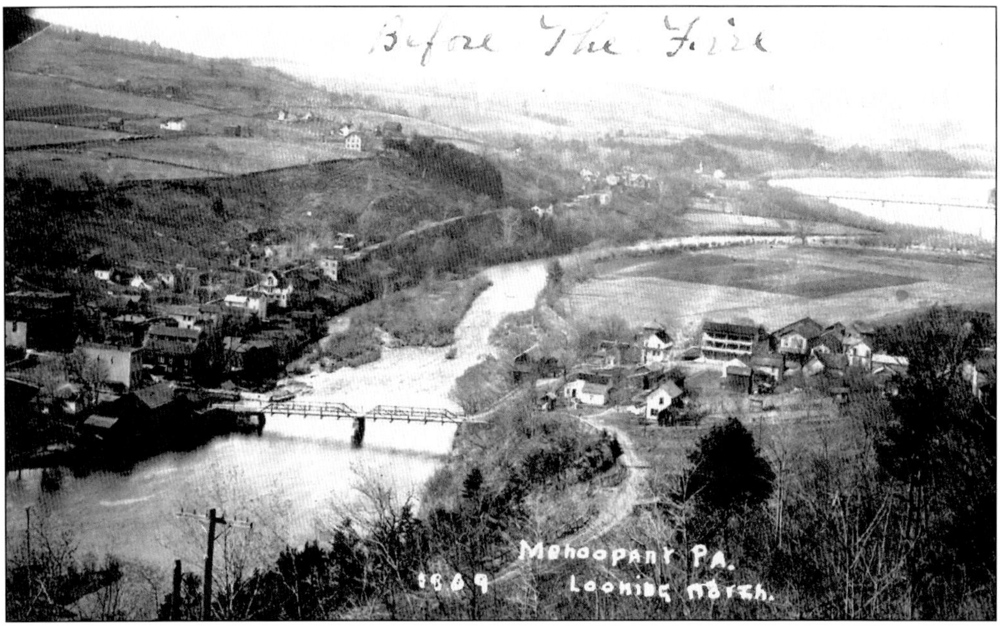

The Susquehanna River and River Bridge can be seen to the right corner of this view of Mehoopany, looking north. The card is postmarked 1914.

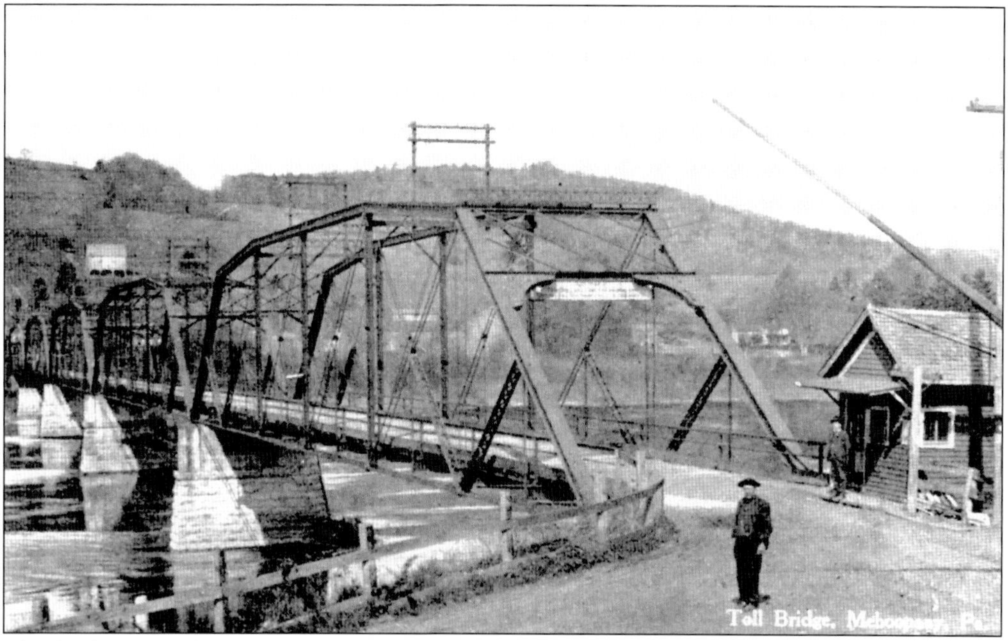

The bridge at Mehoopany crossing the Susquehanna River was originally a toll bridge built in 1899. The county eliminated the tolls when it bought the bridge in 1909.

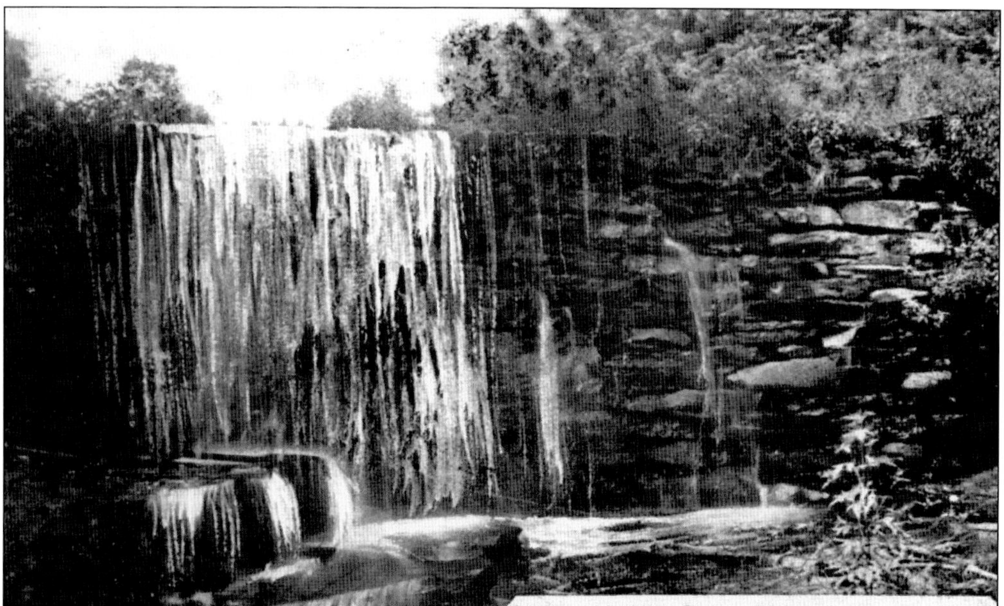

Mehoopany was the home to many mills over the years, including a sawmill owned by the Lotts, and gristmills owned by the Carney, Kintner, and Jennings families.

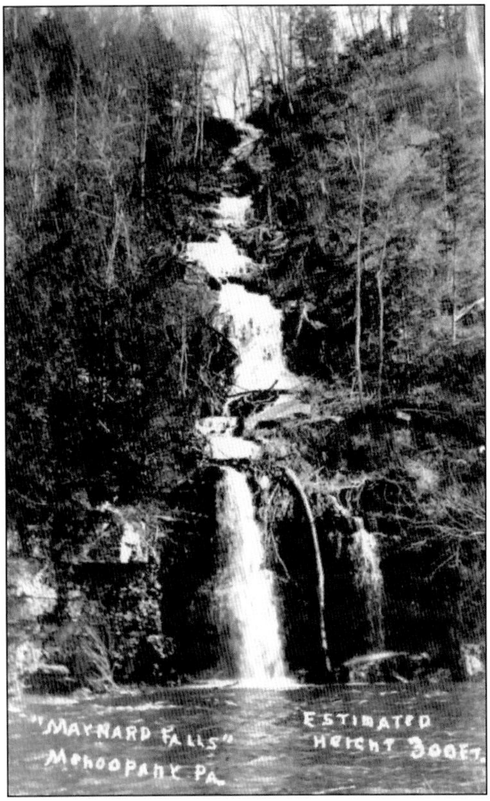

Maynard Falls is located in Mehoopany.

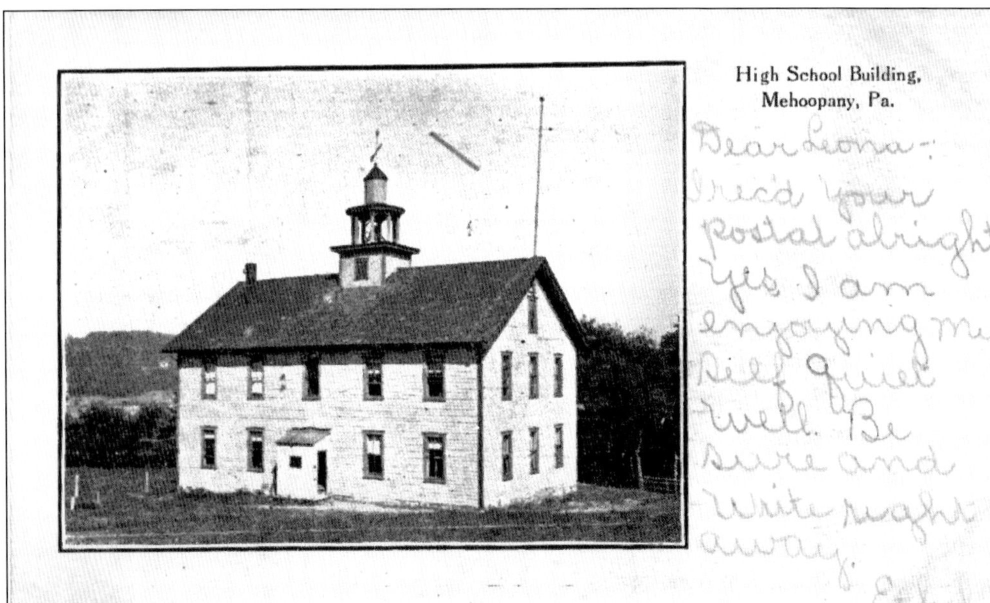

The Mehoopany High School, shown here *c.* 1907, was built in 1884. The bell was added to the belfry in 1886. The school had two rooms upstairs and two rooms downstairs. The last class graduated from this school in 1951. The building is still standing.

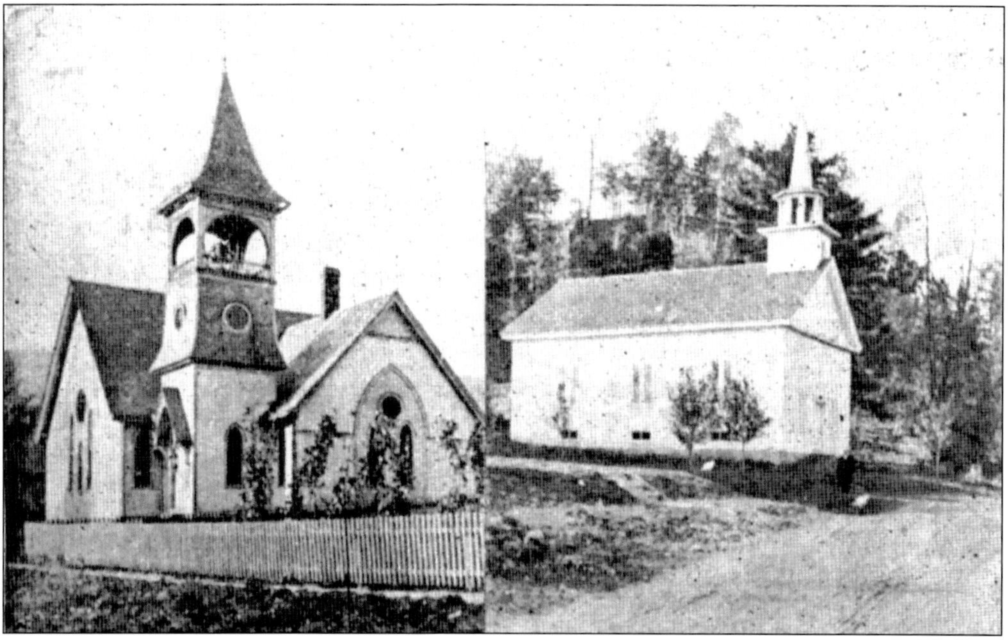

The Mehoopany Presbyterian Church, left, was built in 1891, and the Baptist church was built in 1867. The Baptist church was used until 1967, when the Baptists bought the vacant Presbyterian church. The Baptist church was then torn down.

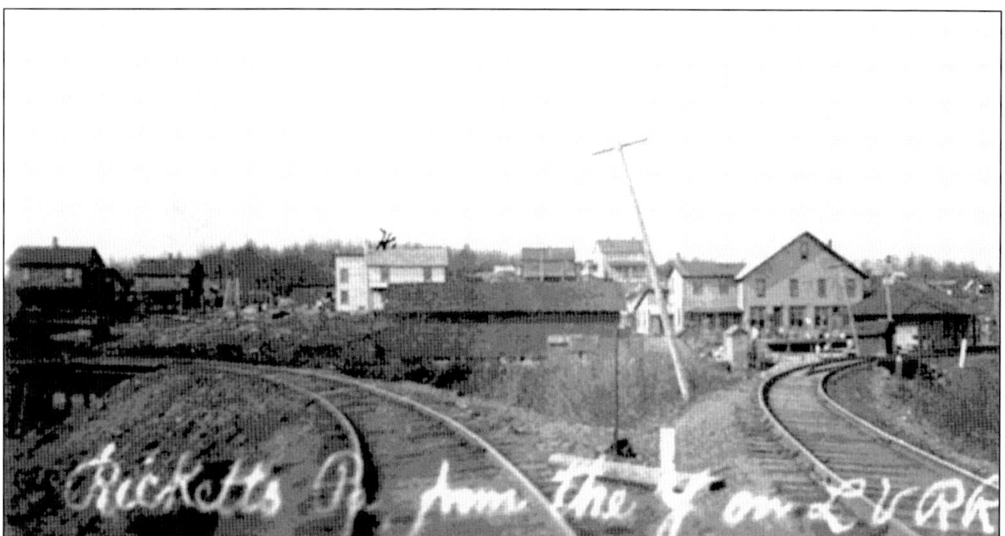

Ricketts was located on the southwest border of Wyoming and Sullivan Counties. The town was named after Col. R. B. Ricketts, who owned most of the land in the area. The town of Ricketts at one time consisted of 150 to 175 dwellings, two schools, a railroad station, a hotel, a Lutheran church, an Irish Catholic church, a doctor, a stave mill, and a spool mill.

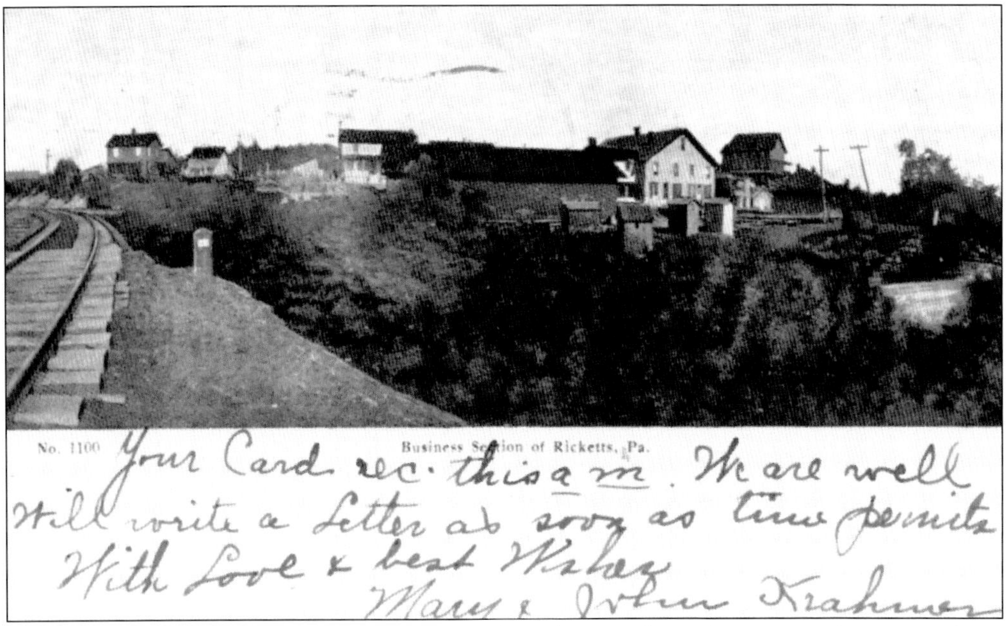

The Lehigh Valley Railroad's Bowman's Creek branch came through Noxen and ran to Ricketts twice daily, once at 9 a.m. and again at 5 p.m.

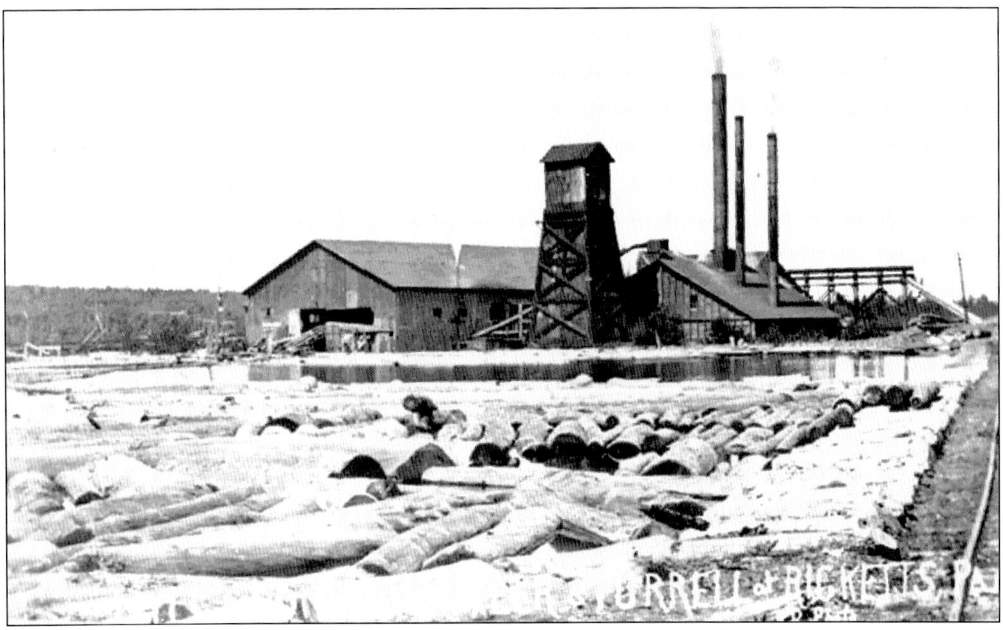

Everyone in Ricketts who worked in the lumber industry worked for the Trexler and Turrell Lumber Company. Founded in 1890, Ricketts became a ghost town after the lumber gave out. Nothing remains of Ricketts today.

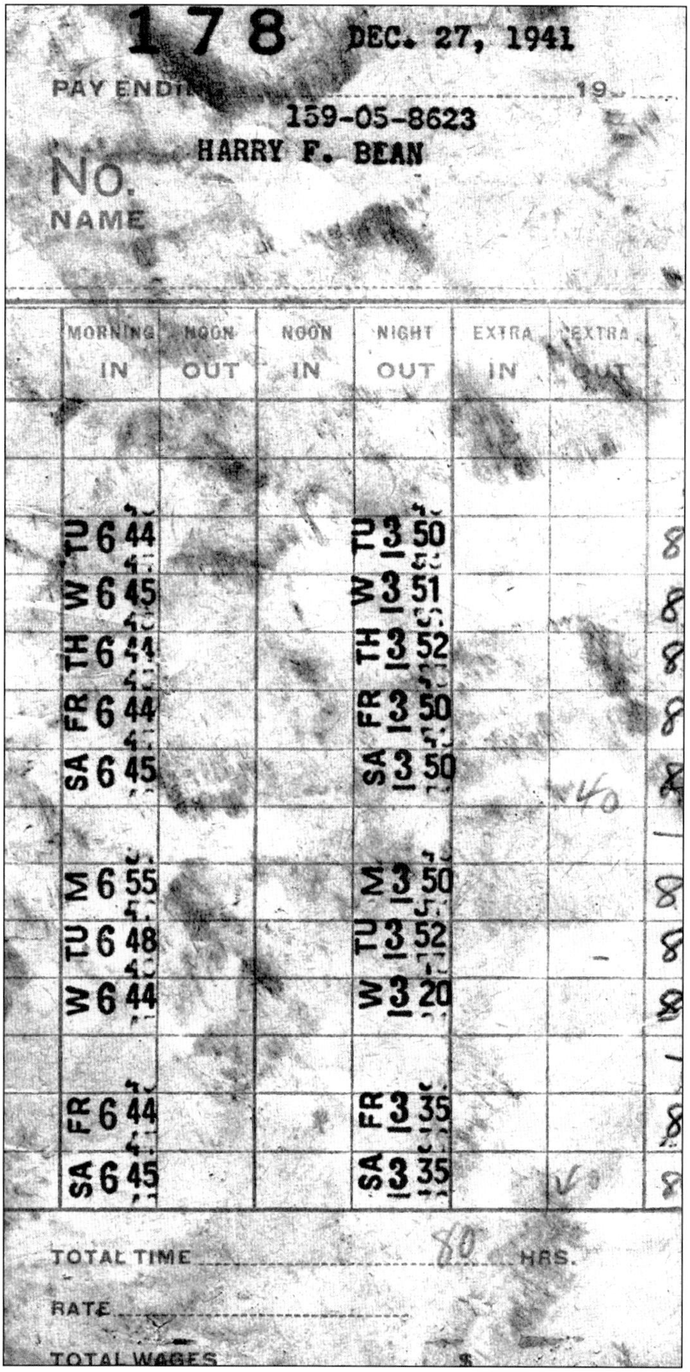

178 DEC. 27, 1941

PAY ENDING .... 19....

159-05-8623

No.

HARRY F. BEAN

NAME

MORNING IN	NOON OUT	NOON IN	NIGHT OUT	EXTRA IN	EXTRA OUT	
TU 6 44			TU 3 50			8
W 6 45			W 3 51			8
TH 6 44			TH 3 52			8
FR 6 44			FR 3 50			8
SA 6 45			SA 3 50			8
M 6 55			M 3 50			8
TU 6 48			TU 3 52			8
W 6 44			W 3 20			8
FR 6 44			FR 3 35			8
SA 6 45			SA 3 35			8

TOTAL TIME ....80........ HRS.

RATE ....

TOTAL WAGES .... $

This is a time card found on the site of the tannery in Noxen in 1981, when it was being torn down. The tannery was built by the Mosser Tanning Company in the 1890s. The tannery received bark needed for tanning from the timberlands of Albert Lewis near Ricketts. The tannery was sold in 1921 to the Armour Company, who ran it until 1961. The building sat idle until 1981, when it was demolished. The site was sold to HUD for low-income housing that was never built. The property is now a baseball field.

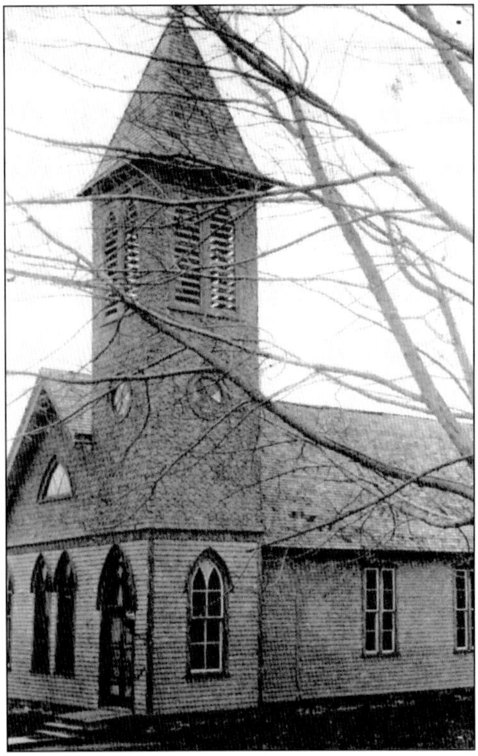

The Methodist Episcopal Church of Noxen was built in 1886 at a cost of $1,000. The church was under the Center Moreland circuit until 1895. This card is postmarked 1907.

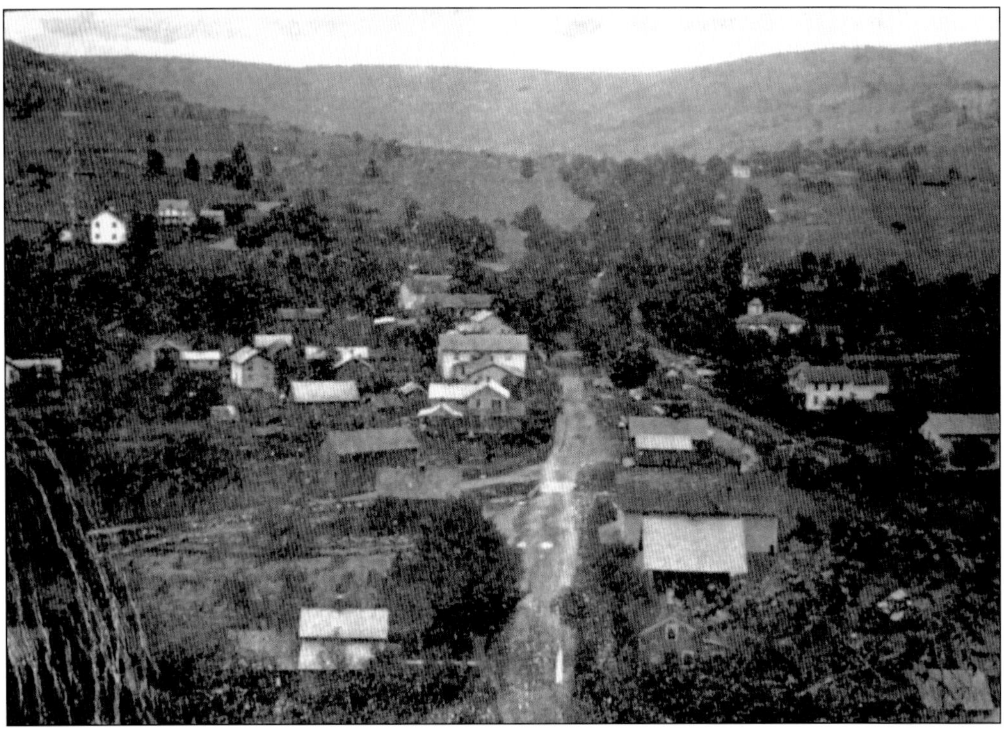

Forkston was named after the fork in the Mehoopany Creek near the village's location. This card is also postmarked 1912.

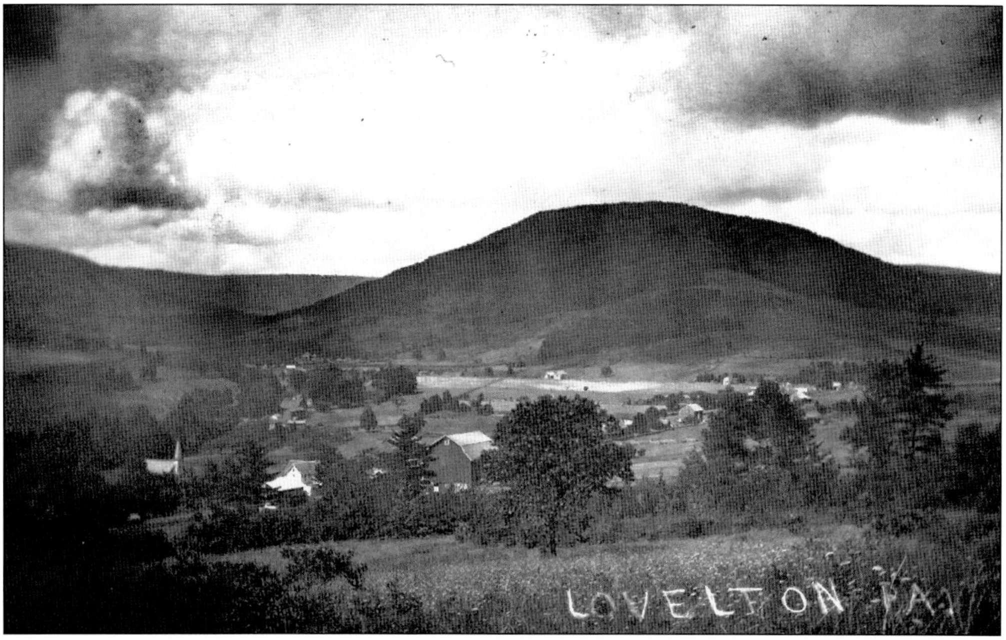

Lovelton was named after an early settler and was the location of the first school and post office in North Branch Township.

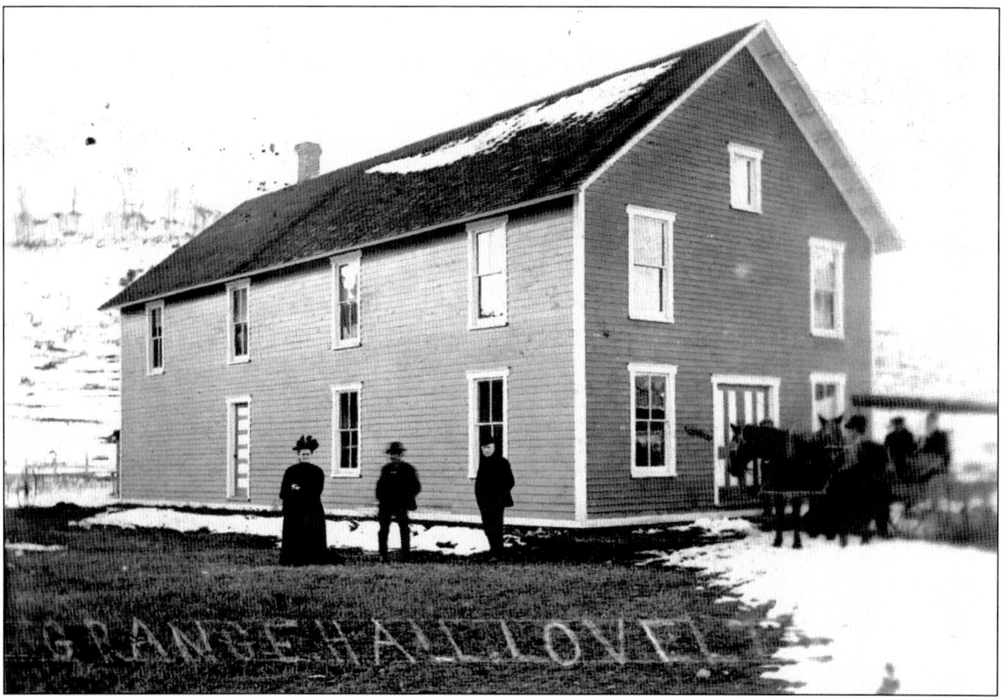

Lovelton Grange Hall was built *c.* 1904 and is still in existence. A porch has been added to the building, but other than that, it looks much the same today. This card is postmarked 1912.

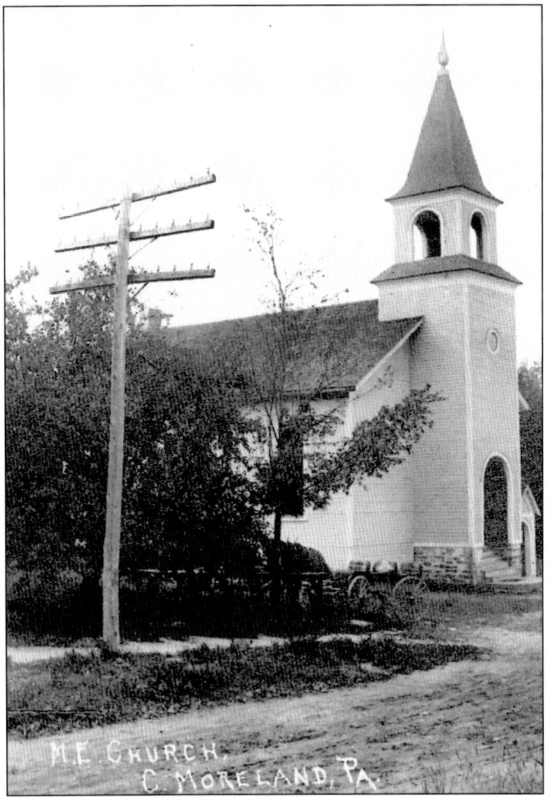

Center Moreland Methodist Episcopal Church, located on Creamery Road, was built in 1870 at a cost of $3,000 to replace the first Methodist church built in 1829. When the church was renovated in 1964, the steeple was removed and the entrance was moved to the side of the building. (Postcard courtesy of Grace DeRemer.)

CHARLES S. BESTEDER,

DEALER IN

...General Merchandise...

DRY GOODS, CLOTHING, HATS AND CAPS,

Groceries, Boots and Shoes,

Hardware, Crockery, Drugs, Notions, Etc.

TELEPHONE PAY STATION.

CENTERMORELAND, PA. r 44 cor. 42.

The Charles S. Besteder store in Center Moreland ran this ad in the *1900 Hanford's Directory of Wyoming County*.

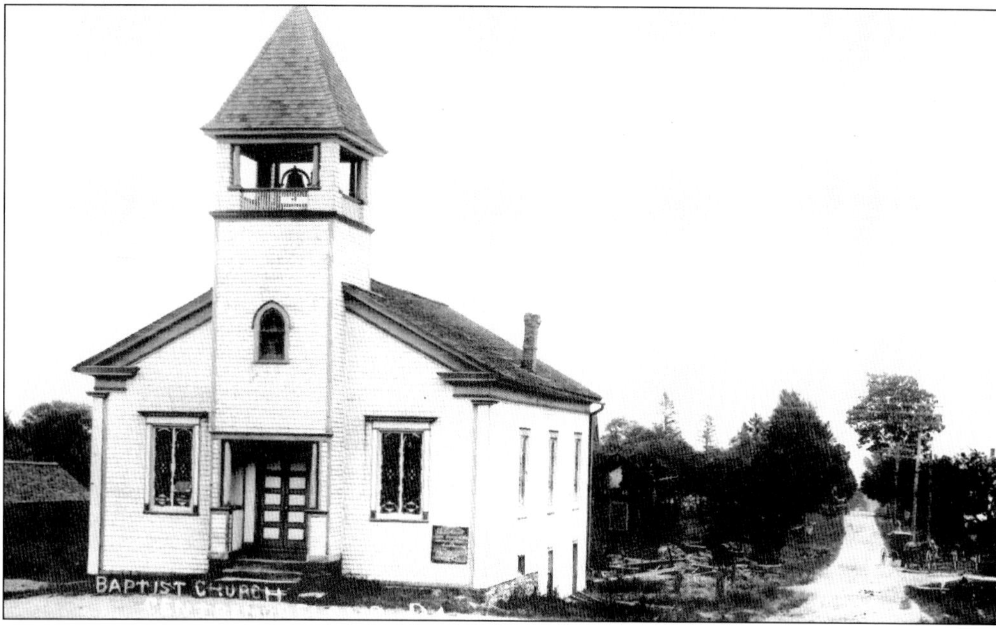

The Center Moreland Baptist Church was first dedicated in 1857. The church, located on Route 292 in Center Moreland, is still active.

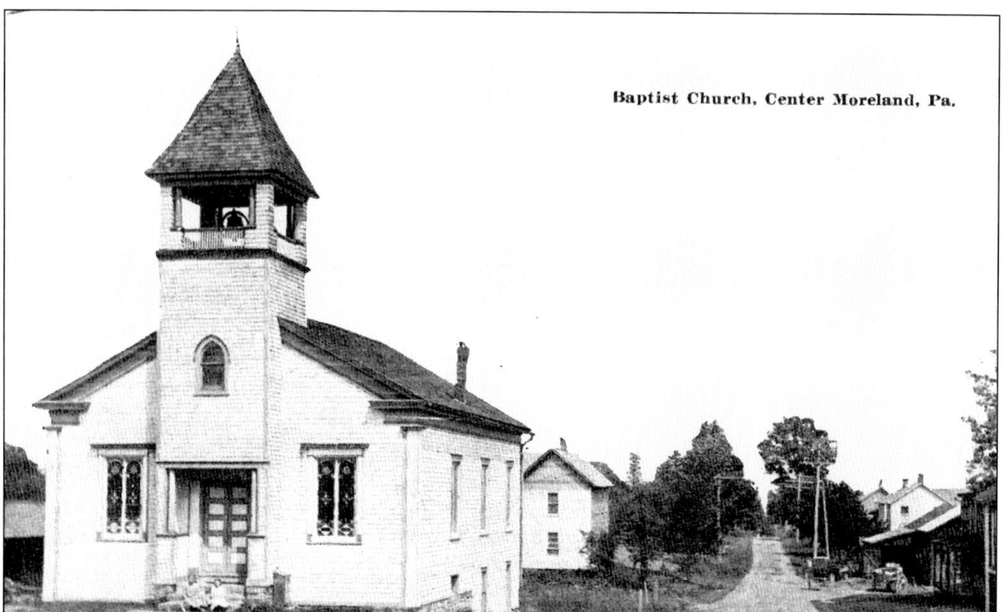

Notice the white house seen in the background of this view of the Center Moreland Baptist Church, postmarked 1912. It is not shown on the previous card because it burned down.

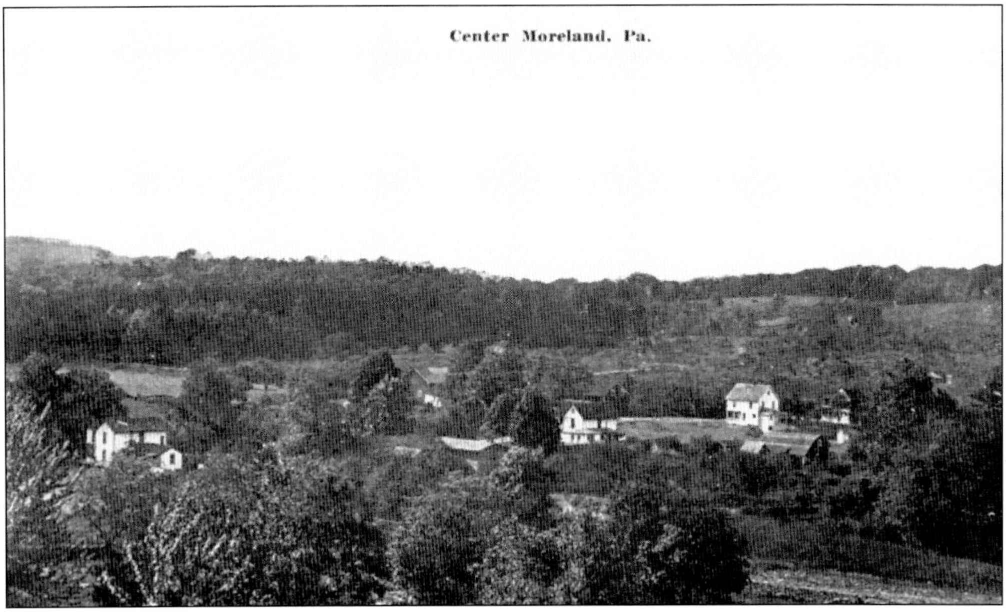

Center Moreland is still surrounded by farmland, much as it was when this postcard was mailed in 1919.

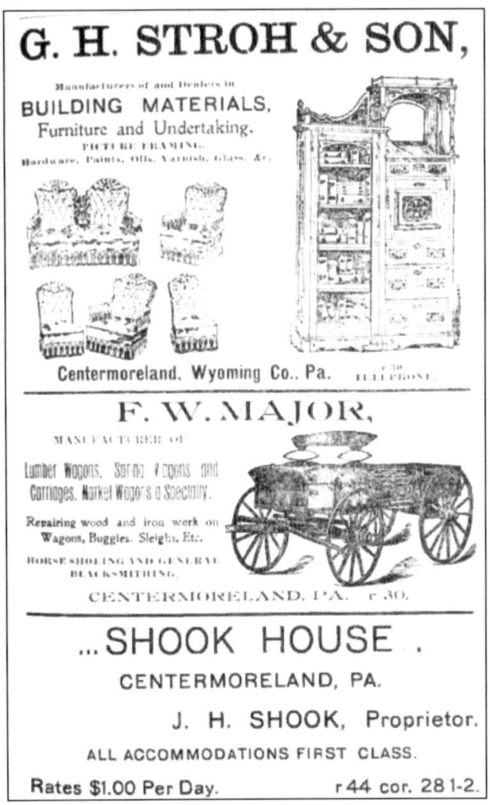

The *1900 Hanford's Directory of Wyoming County* advertised G. H. Stroh & Son, F. W. Major, and the Shook House, all located in Center Moreland.

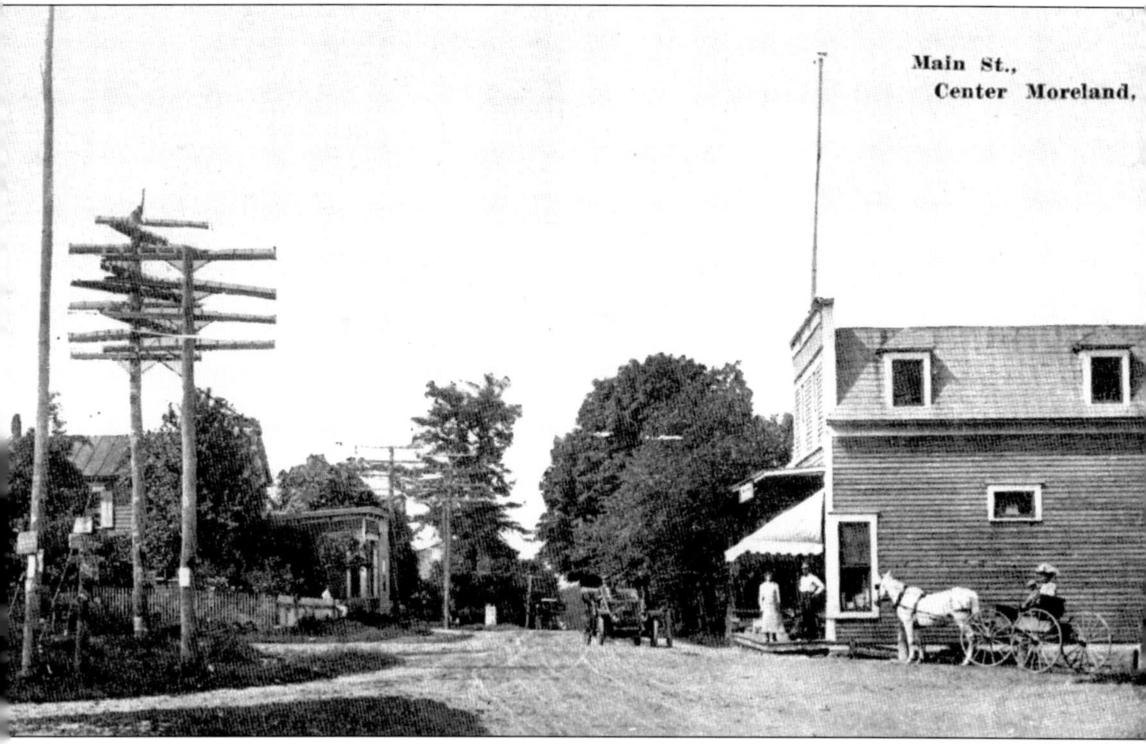

Center Moreland's Main Street was located at what is now the intersection of Route 292 and Demunds Road. In 1908, the Center Moreland post office moved into the store seen to the right. Today, the store operates under the name Centermoreland Grocery and Deli.

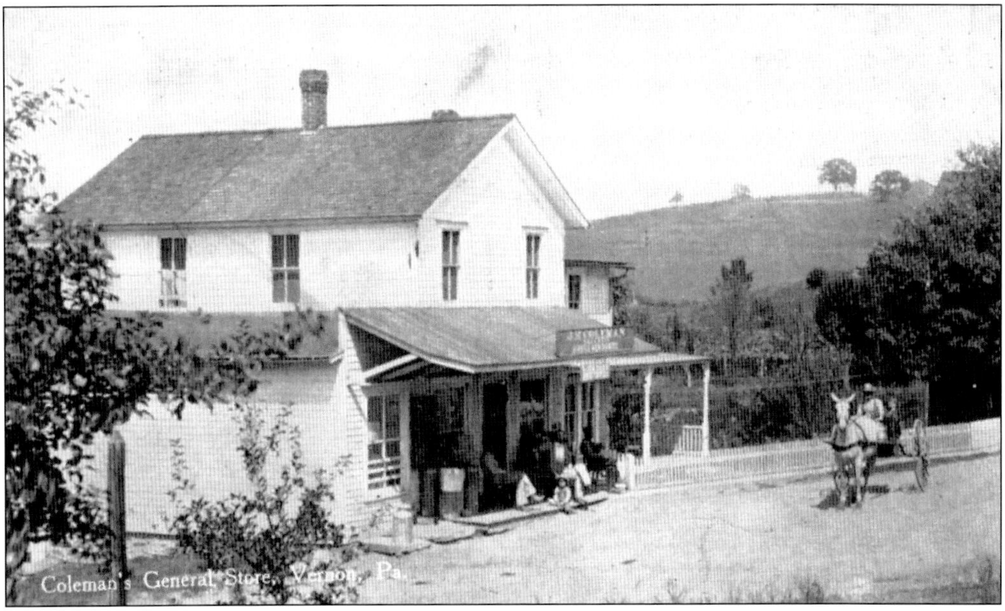

Coleman's Store stood on the corner of the Beaumont to Vernon Road and Route 292. The building was destroyed by fire *c.* 1934, and the site is now the location of a vegetable garden.

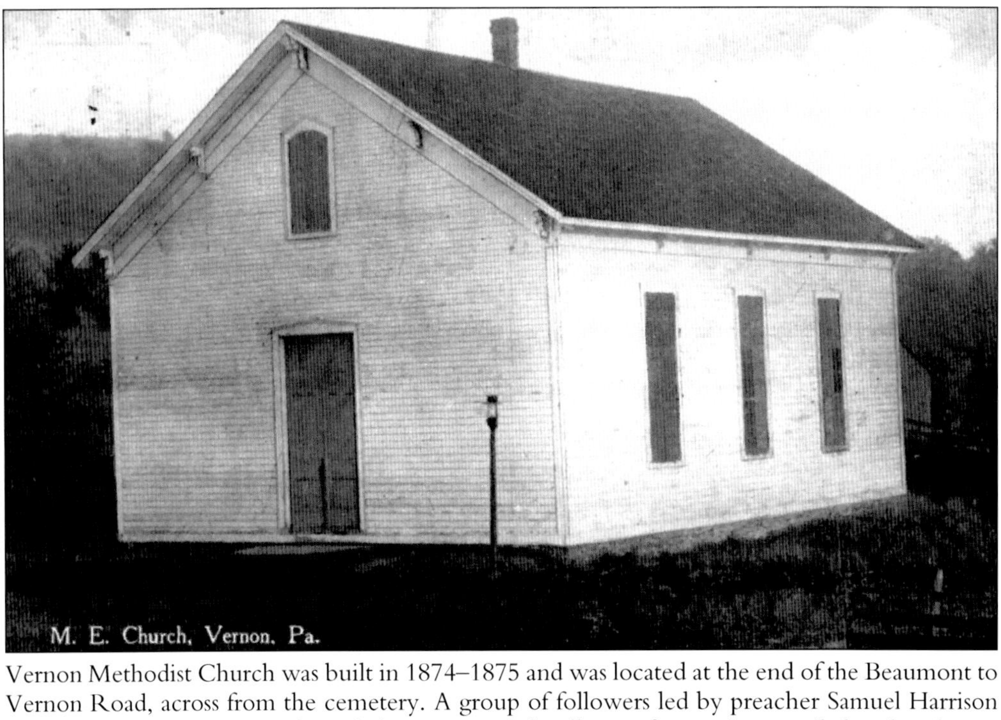

Vernon Methodist Church was built in 1874–1875 and was located at the end of the Beaumont to Vernon Road, across from the cemetery. A group of followers led by preacher Samuel Harrison joined together in 1860 and used the Vernon Schoolhouse for services until the church was built. The building was torn down in the 1950s, and a sawmill was built in its place. The sawmill is now gone.

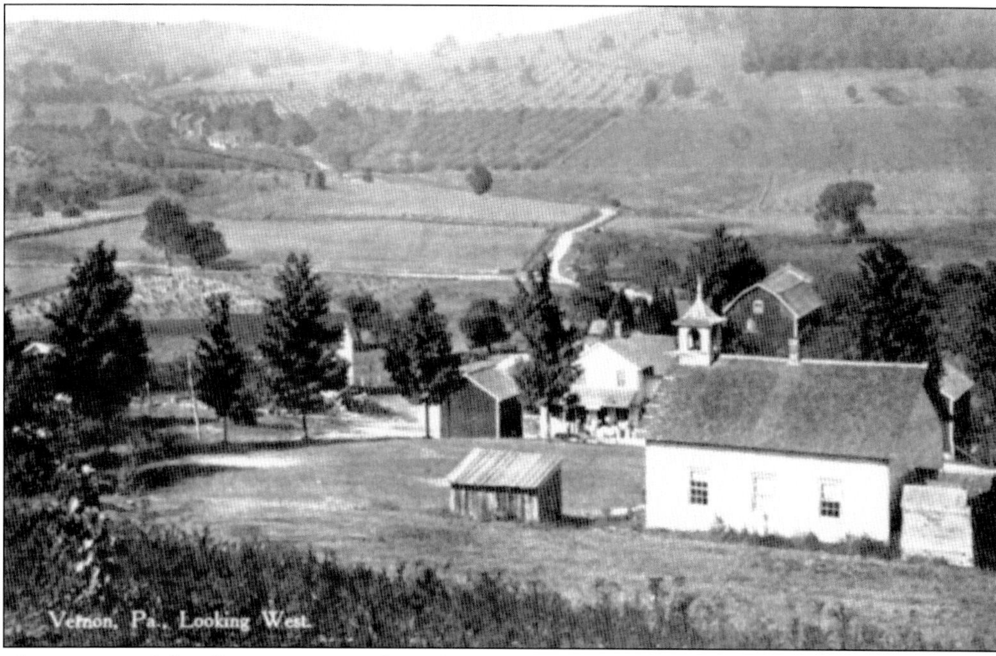

The Vernon Schoolhouse was used until 1954. It was converted into a chicken coop after standing vacant for a number of years. In the 1990s, it was burned down by the fire department. Coleman's Store can be seen in the center past the schoolhouse, and the Methodist church can be seen behind the third tree from the left. Of the buildings shown here, the only ones still standing are the barn above the schoolhouse, and the barns in the far upper left corner.

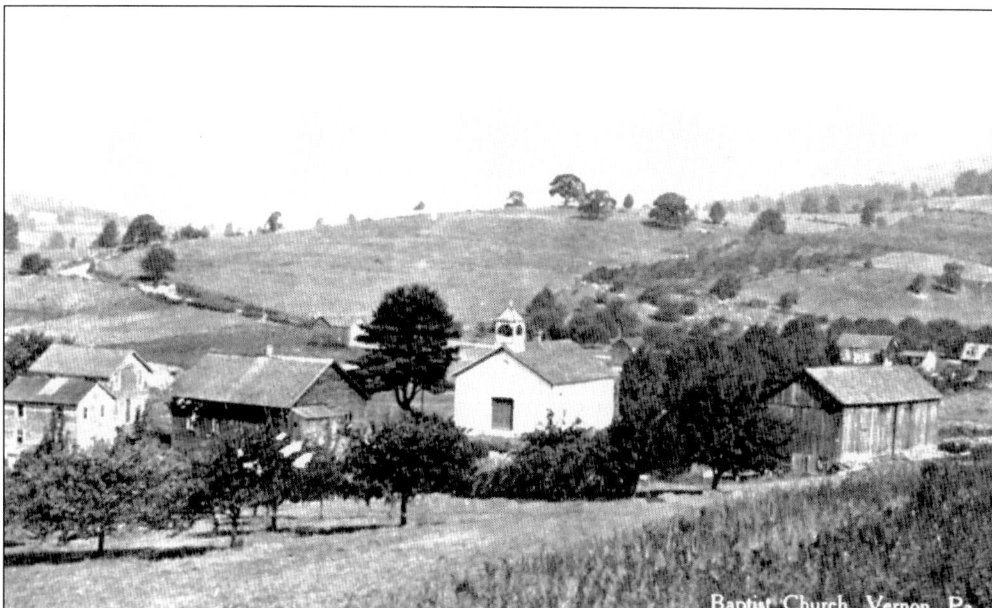

Vernon Baptist Church was built in 1873 by members of the Center Moreland Baptist Church who were looking for a closer place of worship. The church is still active, and the author attended in the 1970s. Lewis DeRemer, who also attended this church, provided valuable history on the Vernon area.

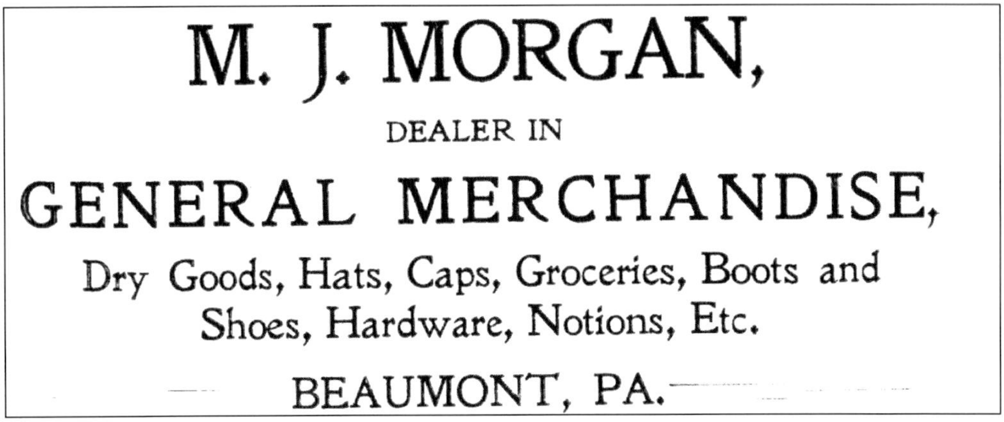

M. J. Morgan's establishment was located in Beaumont according to this ad from the *1900 Hanford's Directory of Wyoming County*.

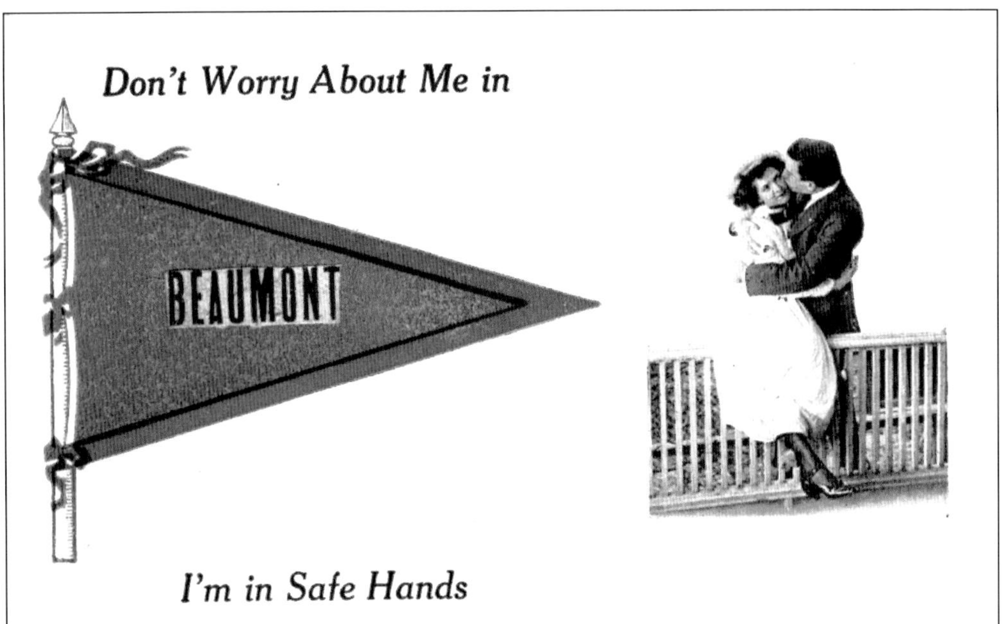

Shown here is a pennant postcard from Beaumont, postmarked 1916. Beaumont postcards are some of the hardest Wyoming County postcards to find, which is surprising in light of the fact that Beaumont is larger than Vernon and other smaller towns from which cards can be found.

BEAUMONT HOUSE,

WILLARD RACE, Propr.

Rates one dollar per day. First class accommodations for guests. Also Livery and stabling in Connection.

MAIN STREET, BEAUMONT, WYOMING CO., PA.

The *1900 Hanford's Directory of Wyoming County* advertised the Beaumont House on Main Street in Beaumont when Willard Race was the proprietor.

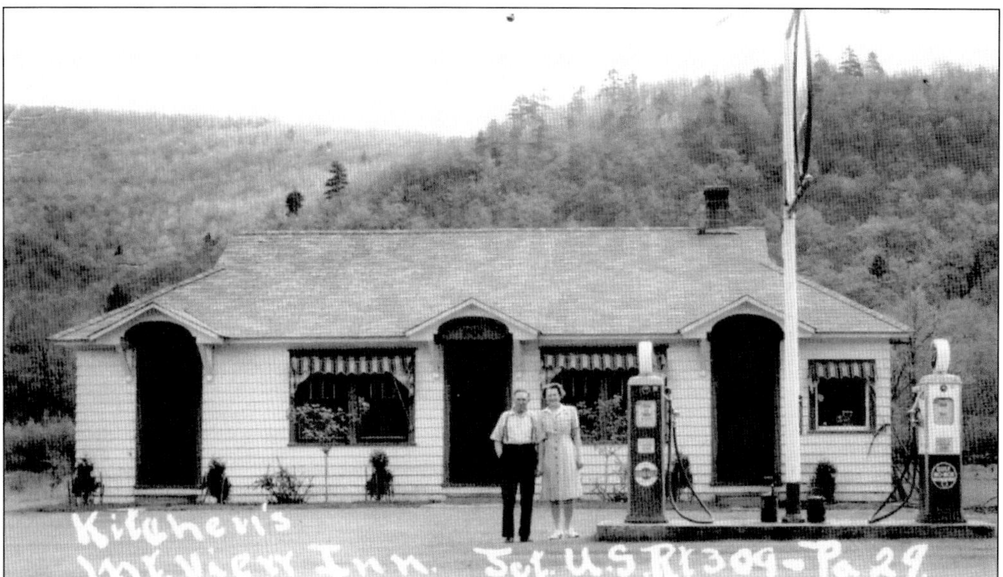

This card shows Kitchen's Mountain View Inn, located at the junction of U.S. Route 309 and Pennsylvania Route 29. The building existed through the 1980s and was, at one point, a dress factory. The only thing currently left of the original gas station is a Gulf gas sign. A small plaza is located on the site now.

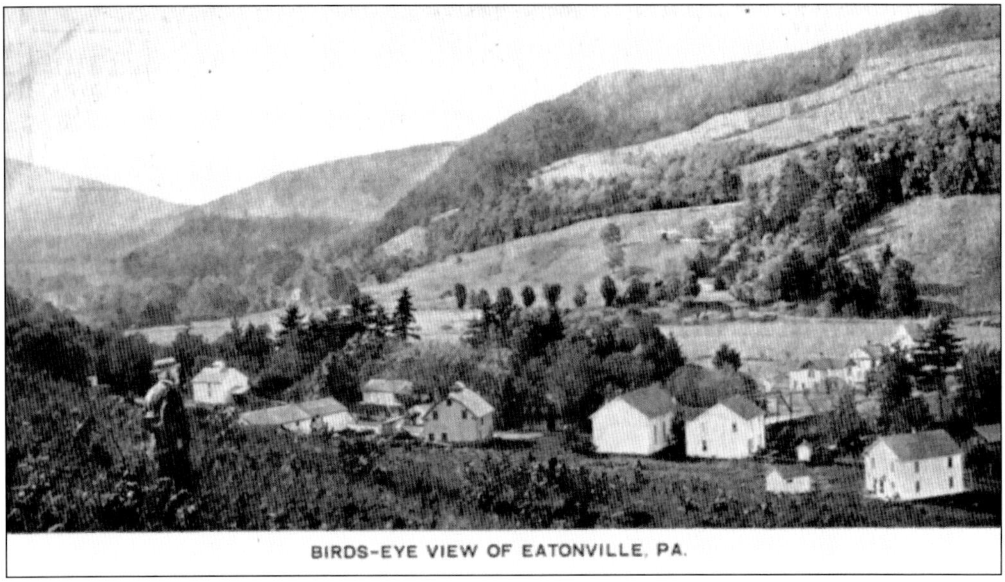

In this view of Eatonville, the iron bridge can be seen toward the right.

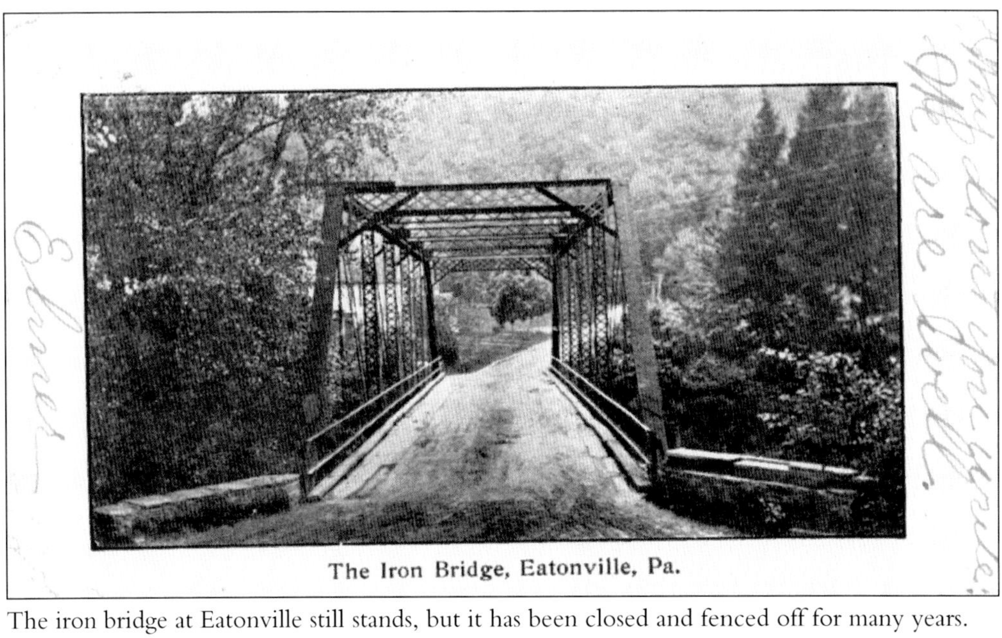

The iron bridge at Eatonville still stands, but it has been closed and fenced off for many years.

Four

The Eastern Edge of the County

Clinton Township was formed on February 20, 1844. The first part of the township to be settled was the area that became Factoryville. The borough was formed from Clinton Township on November 12, 1883. The first post office in Factoryville was established in 1828 with Dr. John Wilson as postmaster. The name Factoryville was chosen because of a cotton mill that operated in the area for a short time during the 1820s.

Exeter Township was named after Exeter, Rhode Island, and like its namesake, it is relatively small. One of the original townships, it became a cottage community along the Susquehanna River.

Falls Township was named for the waterfalls on Buttermilk Creek and was formed from Tunkhannock Township in 1824. When the North Branch Canal was in operation, Falls consisted of seven stores, two taverns, a tannery, a gristmill, a sawmill, and other businesses. Mill City, also located in Falls Township, was founded by Chauncey Sherwood. A post office was established in 1865, and the postmaster was Stephen O. Corwin.

Nicholson Township was formed in 1794 and was originally called Thornbottom. Early settlers were mostly interested in the lumber. A sawmill was first built on the Tunkhannock Creek in this area in 1793 by Eliphalet S. and Ebenezer Stevens. The Nicholson post office was established in 1855, and the borough was incorporated in 1875.

Overfield Township, founded in 1859, was taken from Falls and Clinton Townships and contains the village of Lake Winola.

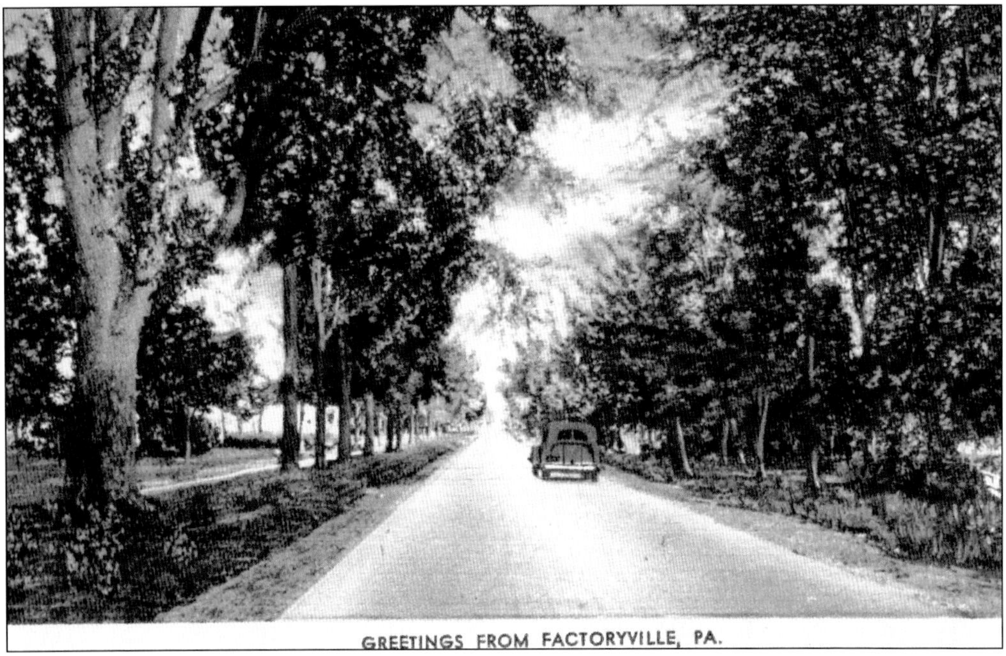

Factoryville became a borough in 1883. It was the first area settled in Clinton Township, and its first post office was established in 1828. This card is postmarked 1916.

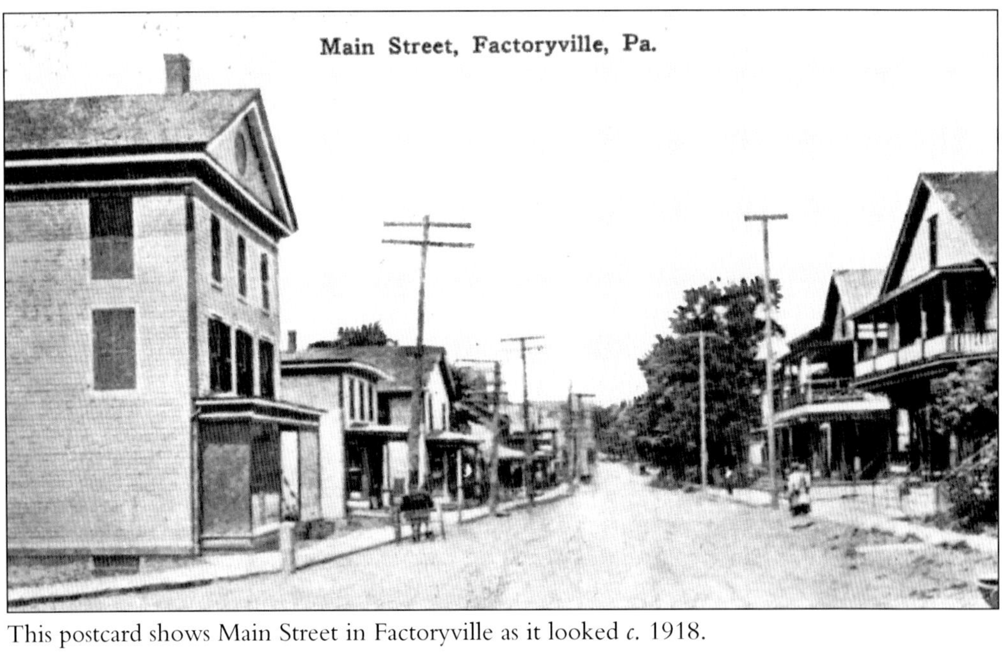

This postcard shows Main Street in Factoryville as it looked *c.* 1918.

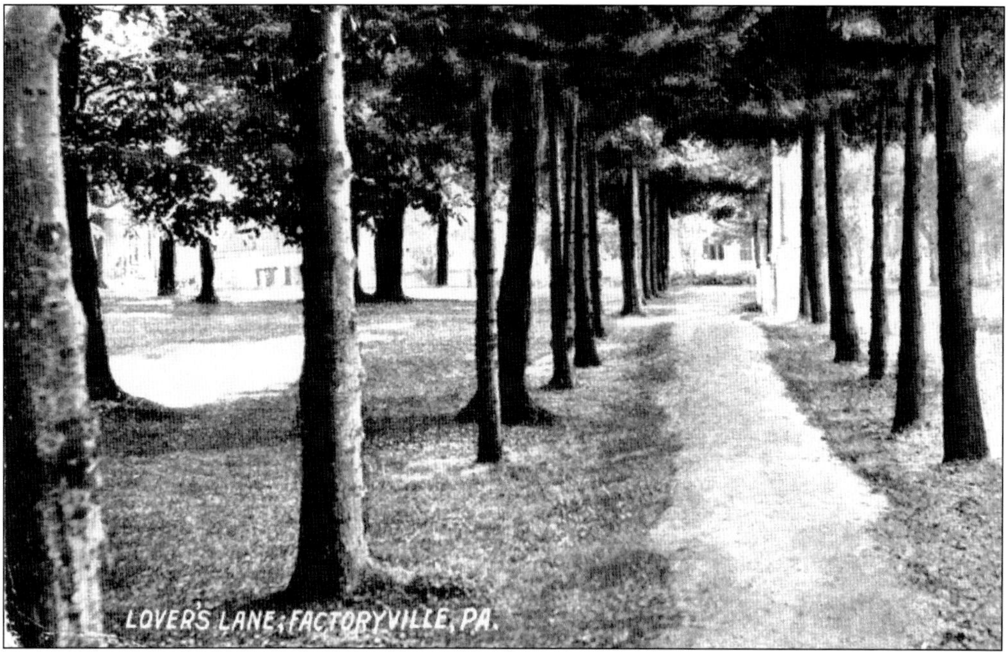

Like Meshoppen, Factoryville also had a lovers' lane.

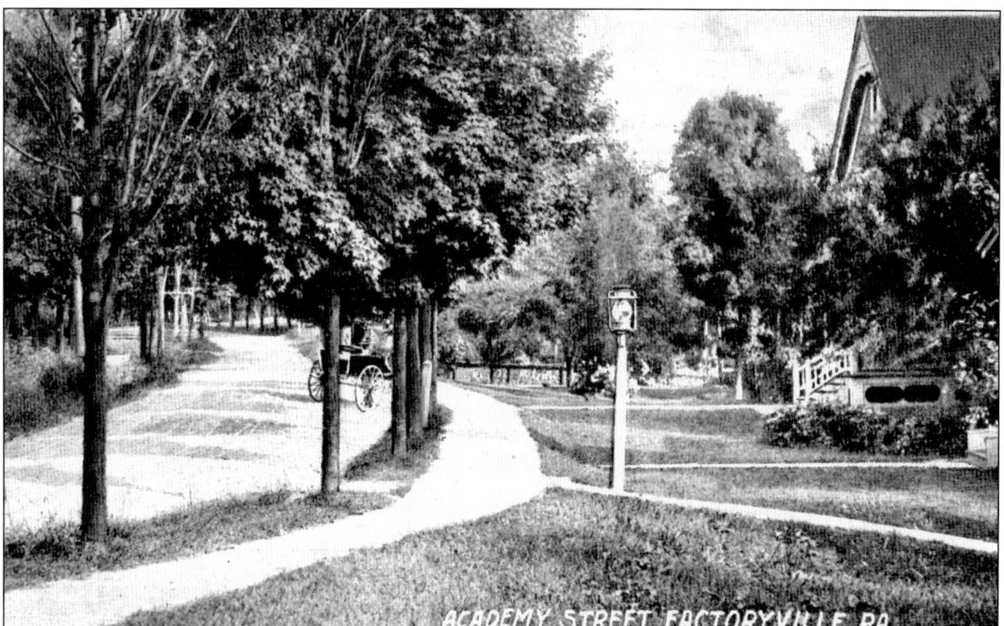

Academy Street was named for Keystone Academy, founded in 1869. Notice the buggy on the street and the gas lamp next to the sidewalk.

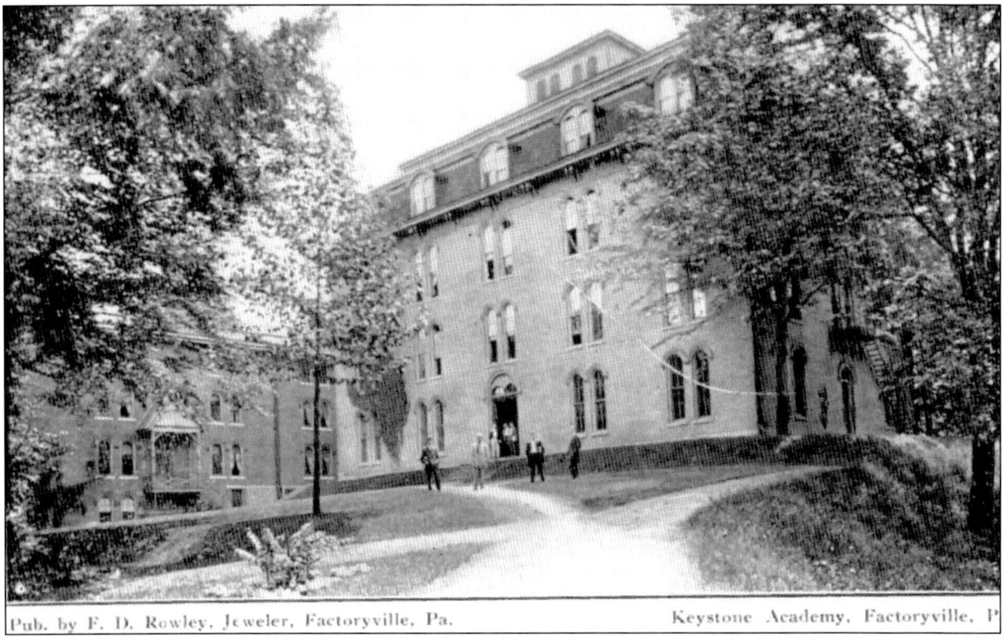

Keystone Academy was started by citizens of Factoryville to educate young people and prepare them for a profession. The first classes were held in Factoryville Baptist Church. Shown here is the first building, Harris Hall, built in 1871. In 1934, the academy became a junior college, which is still in operation as the only college in Wyoming County.

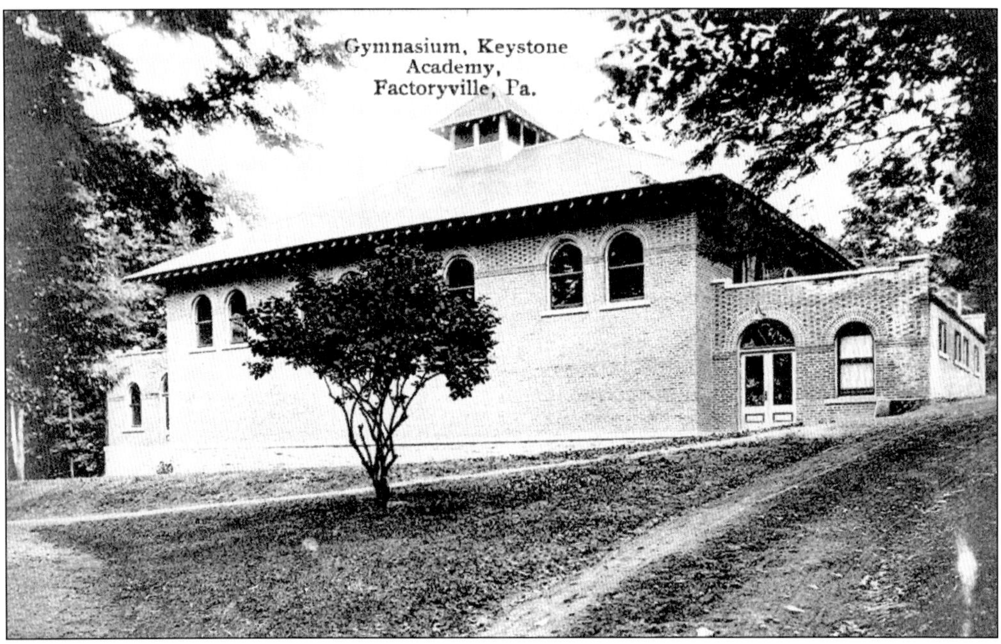

Started on 21 acres, the academy expanded to more than 10 times that size. The gymnasium shown here is now an art center.

KEYSTONE ACADEMY

PREPARES FOR ALL THE LEADING

COLLEGES, UNIVERSITIES AND TECHNICAL SCHOOL

IN THE UNITED STATES.

It also offers a one year's Commercial Course and a three year's Bus ness Course and graduates pupils in Music.

The teachers are College Trained Specialists. There is an exceptional fine campus of twenty acres. There is also mountain spring water a through the buildings.

For full particulars, send for catalogue to

Rev. ELKANAH HULLEY, A. M., Principal,
FACTORYVILLE, PA.

The school not only prepared students for colleges and universities, but it had "mountain spring water all through the buildings," according to this ad from the *1900 Hanford's Directory of Wyoming County*.

CHARLES GARDNER,

DEALER IN

Dry Goods, Groceries, Crockery, Glassware

Hardware, Iron and Farming Implements, Etc.

OILS, PAINTS, VARNISHES, DEERING HAR-
VESTING MACHINERY.

In 1900, merchants such as Charles Gardner, who advertised in the *1900 Hanford's Directory of Wyoming County,* had to carry as much inventory as possible for their customers because traveling to the larger cities was difficult.

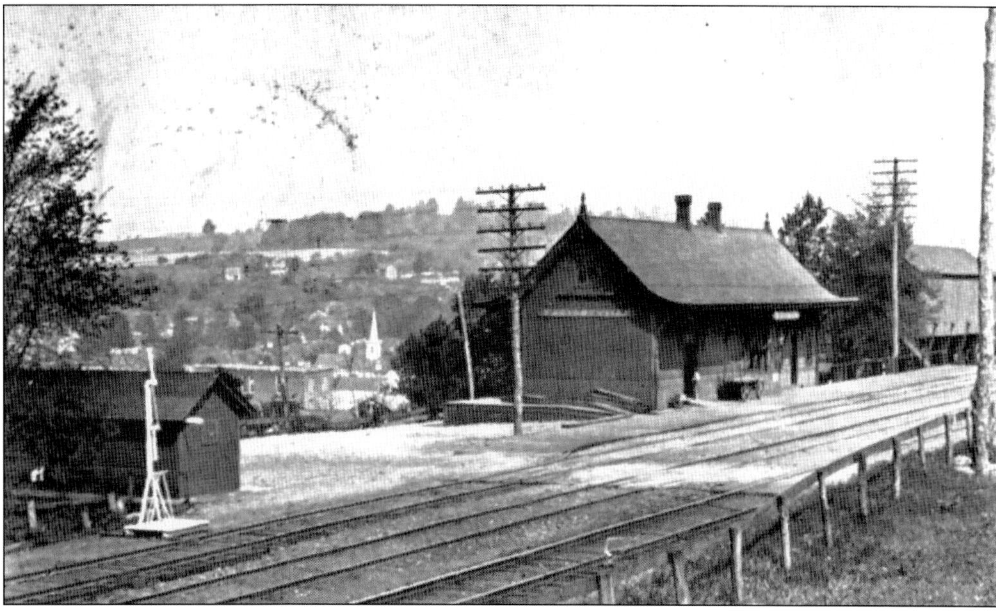

The Delaware, Lackawanna & Western station in Factoryville traces its history back to 1832, with the incorporation of the Ligett's Gap Railroad that ran from Scranton to Hallstead, New York, through Factoryville and Nicholson. The railroad changed its name to the Lackawanna and Western in 1851 and merged with the Delaware and Cobb's Gap Railroad in 1853 to become the Delaware, Lackawanna & Western. After passenger traffic ended on the Delaware, Lackawanna & Western, the station was used as a restaurant until it burned in 1988. This card is postmarked 1909.

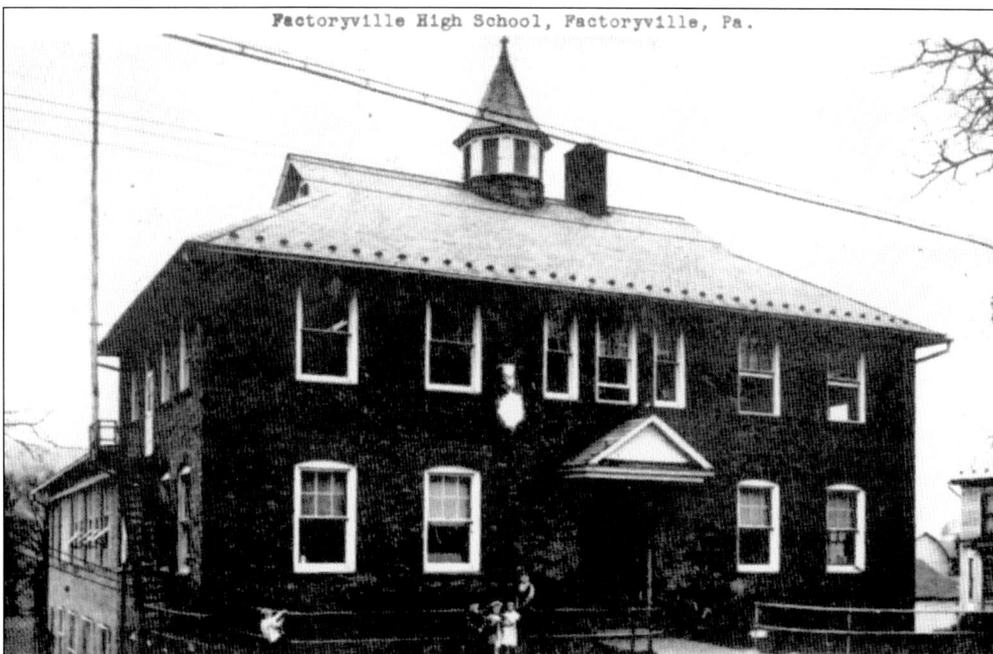

The first high school in Factoryville was built in 1890. The second one, shown here, was built in 1909.

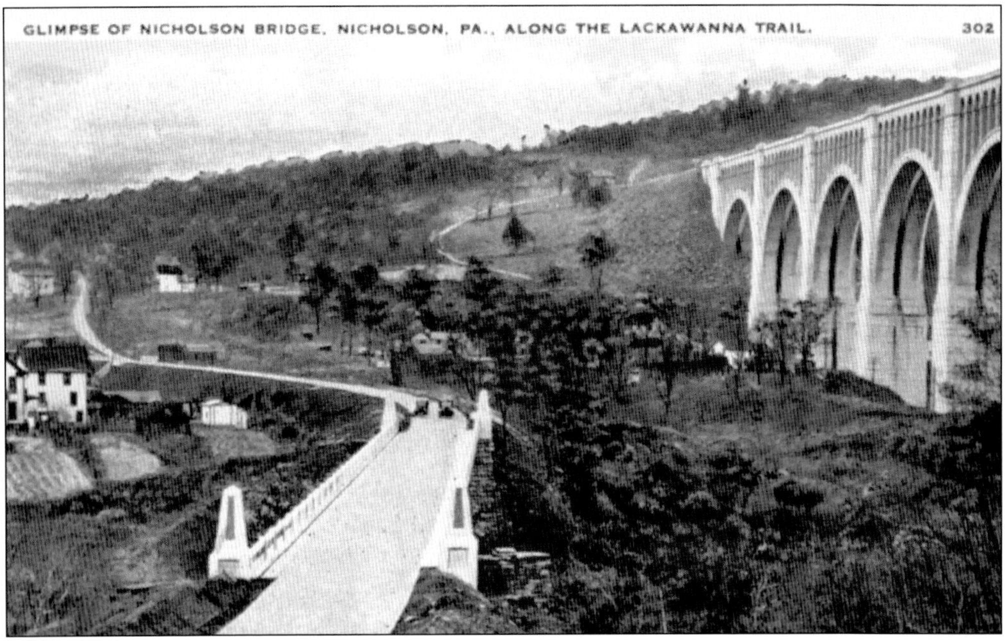

The Tunkhannock Viaduct was built by the Delaware, Lackawanna & Western Railroad to cross the Tunkhannock Creek in Nicholson and cut three miles off the length of the line. The automobile bridge in the postcard was removed and a new bridge was built to the right of the one shown.

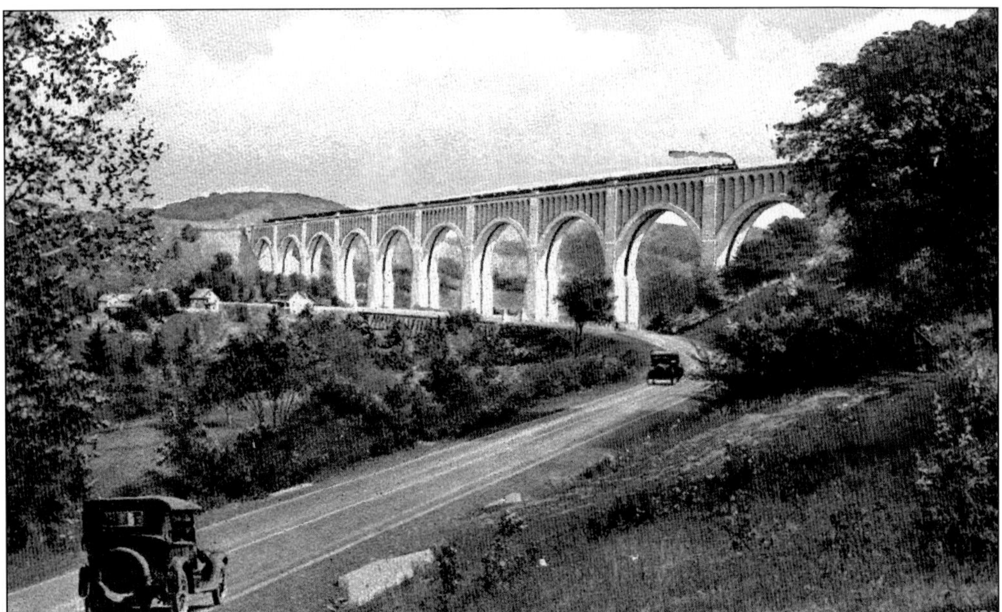

Construction on the Tunkhannock Viaduct (also known as the Nicholson Bridge) began in 1912, and the bridge was dedicated in 1915. The bridge contains 167,000 cubic yards of concrete and 1,000 tons of reinforcing steel.

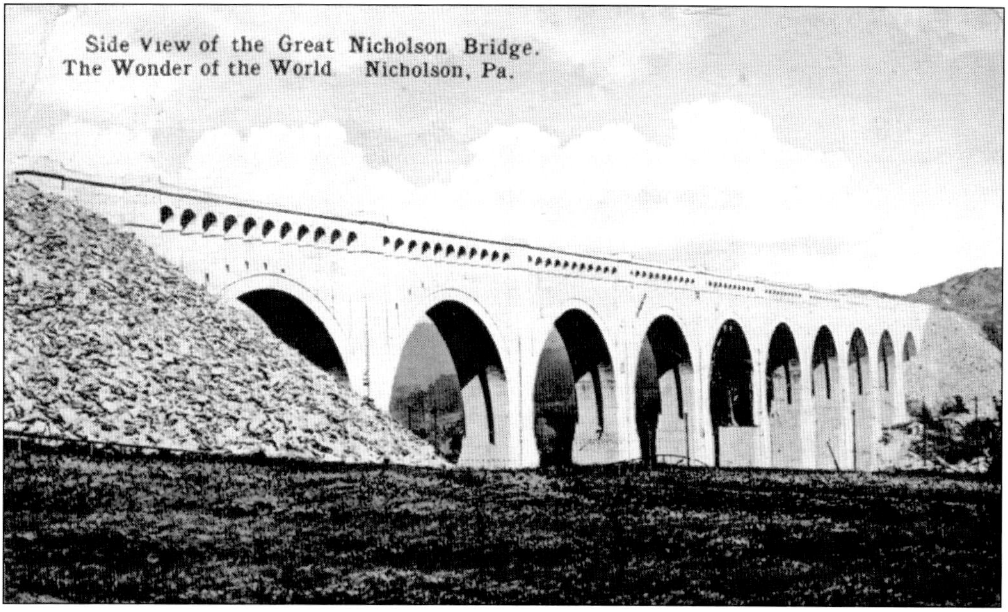

The Tunkhannock Viaduct, shown here *c.* 1924, has been called a wonder of the modern world. The bridge is 2,375 feet long and is 240 feet above the Tunkhannock Creek.

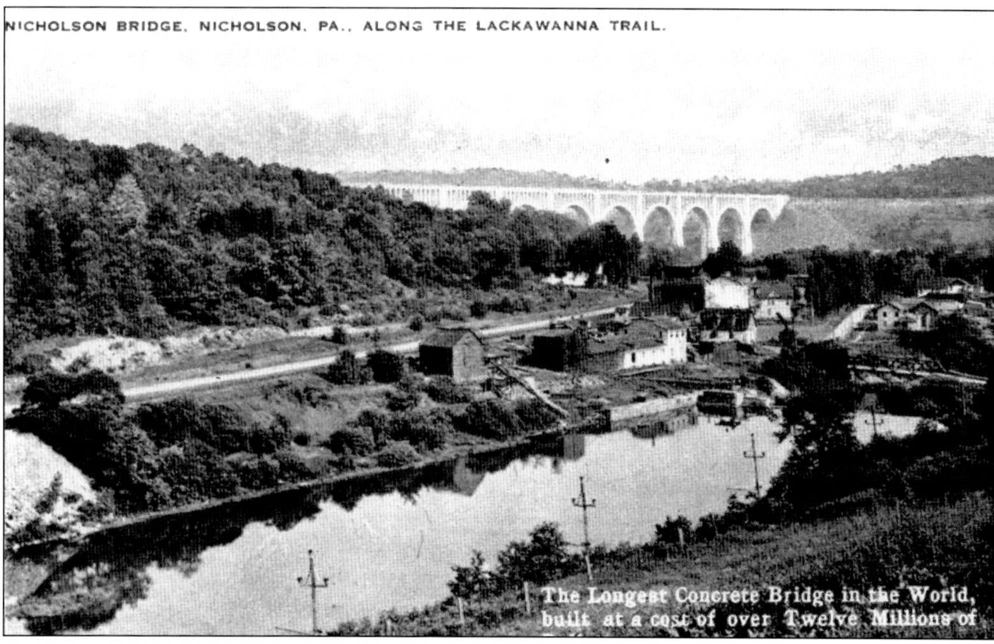

In 1916, author Theodore Dreiser saw the bridge and wrote, "As before the great cathedral at Rheims or Amiens or Canterbury, or those giant baths in Rome which so gratify the imagination, so here at Nicholson, in a valley celebrated for nothing in particular and at the edge of a town of no size, we stood before this vast structure, gazing in a sort of awe."

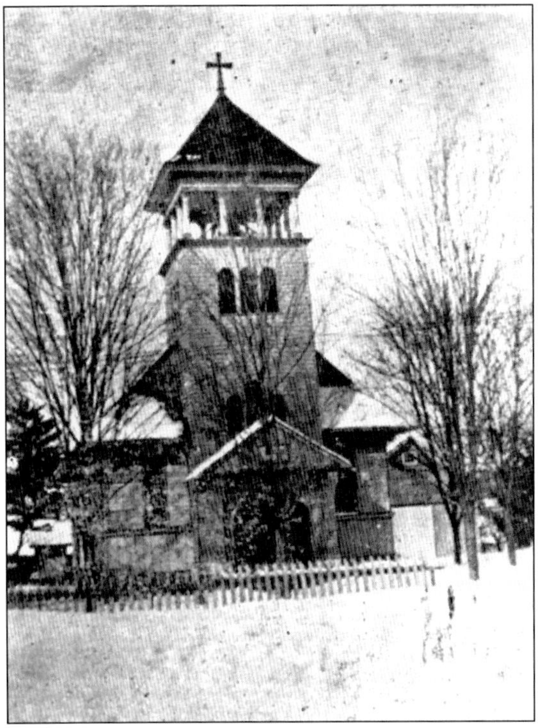

St. Patrick's Church in Nicholson was located on High Street and built in 1891. It is the second church; the first one was located on Main Street and was destroyed by fire in 1890. The card is postmarked 1907.

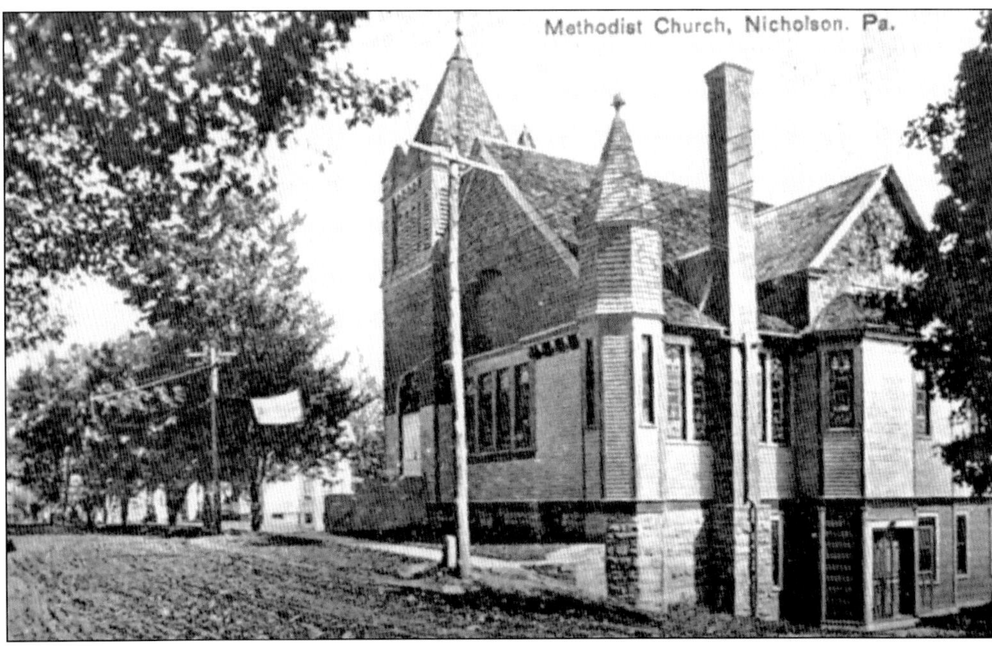

The Methodist church in Nicholson was built in 1903 on State Street. The church, located almost across from the Presbyterian church, still looks much the same today as it does in this card, postmarked 1934.

The Presbyterian church in Nicholson was built in 1869 on State Street.

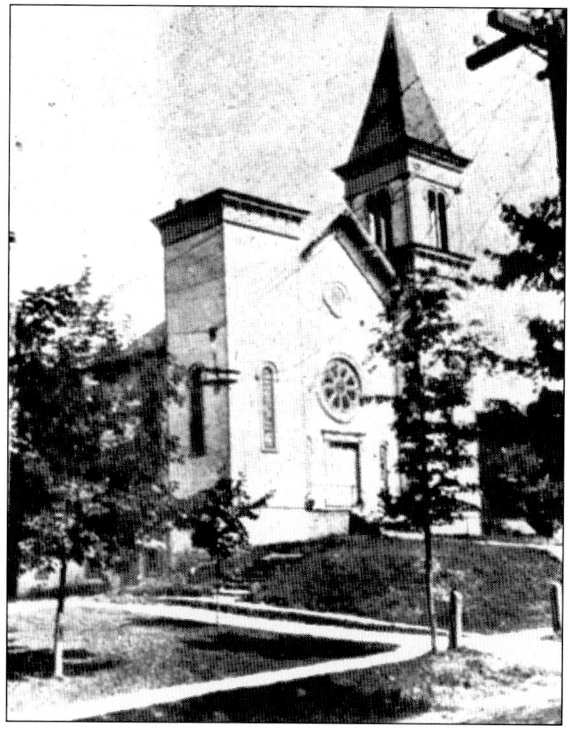

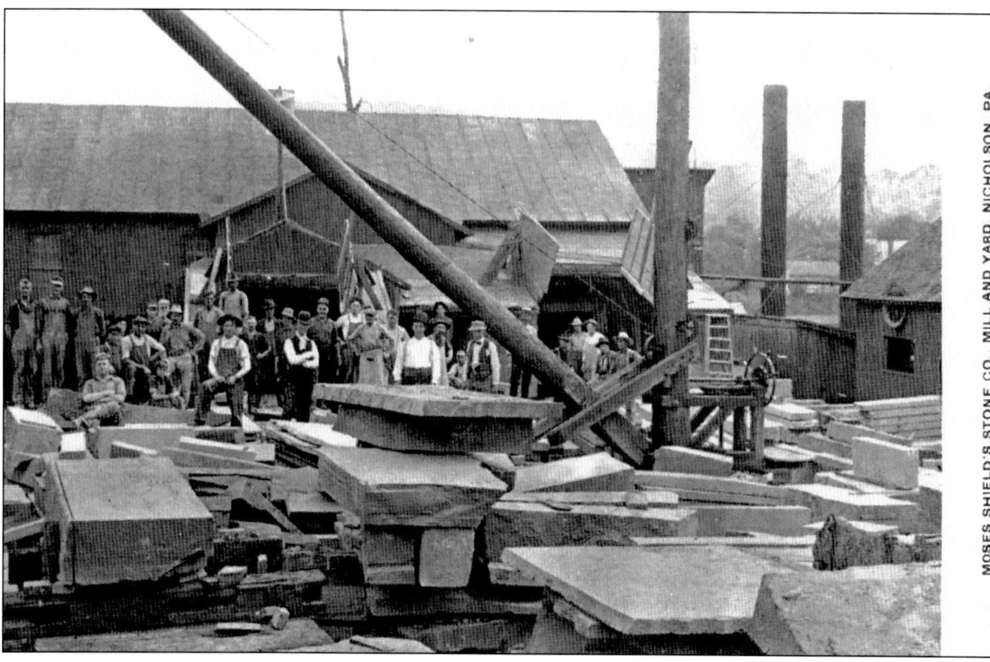

Moses Shield's stone company was located in Nicholson on what is now Route 11. The area is currently the site of the Pump n' Pantry. This card is postmarked 1911.

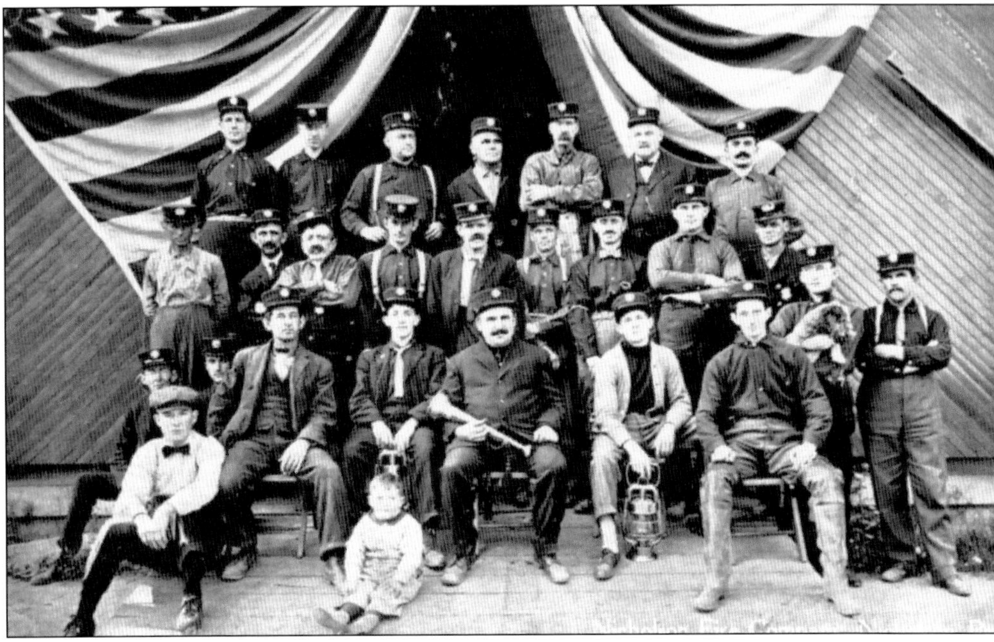

The Nicholson Fire Company was formed in 1904 after a fire destroyed 20 buildings in town.

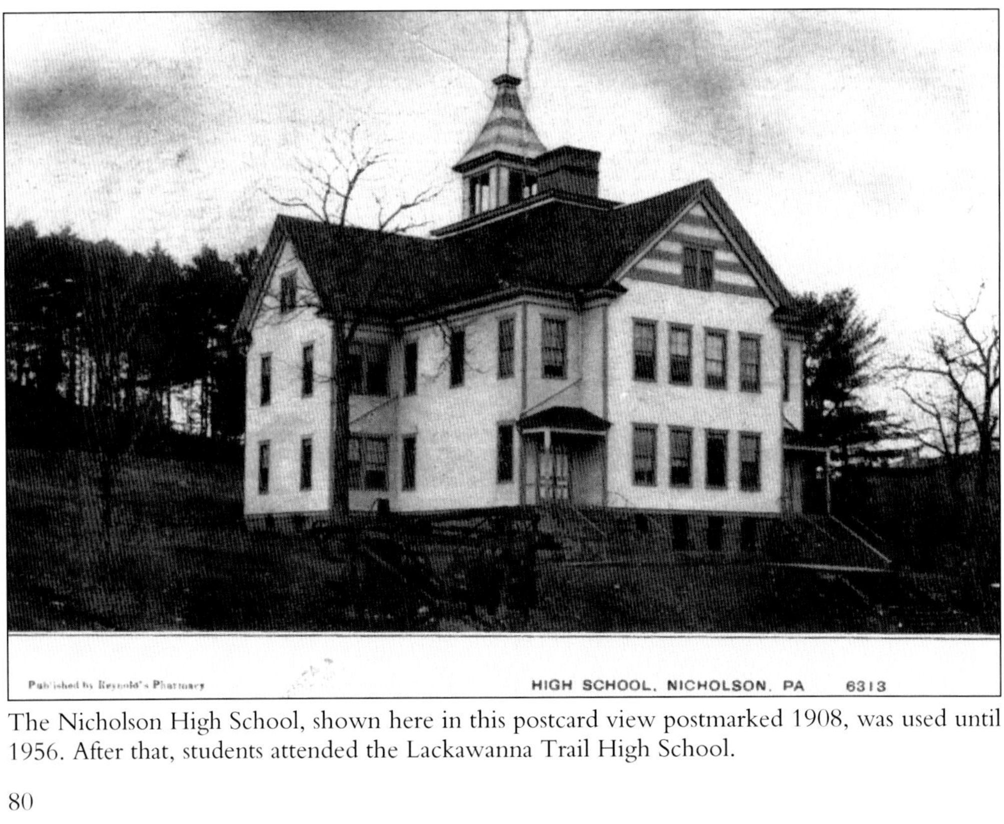

The Nicholson High School, shown here in this postcard view postmarked 1908, was used until 1956. After that, students attended the Lackawanna Trail High School.

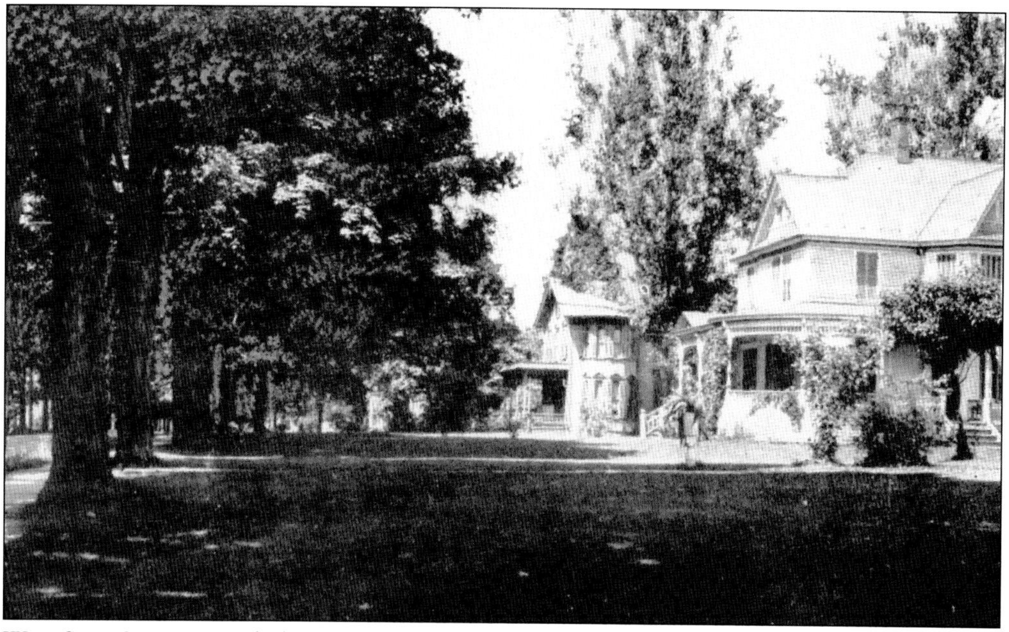

West State Street in Nicholson looks much the same today as it does in this postcard view, with large Victorian homes sitting back from the street, providing large front lawns.

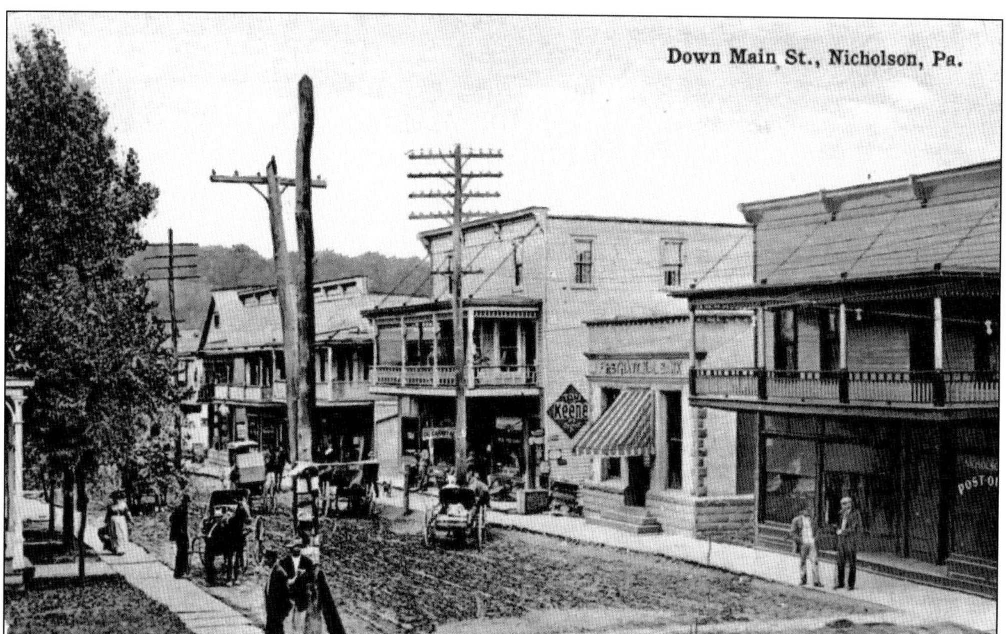

This view of Main Street in Nicholson includes the post office.

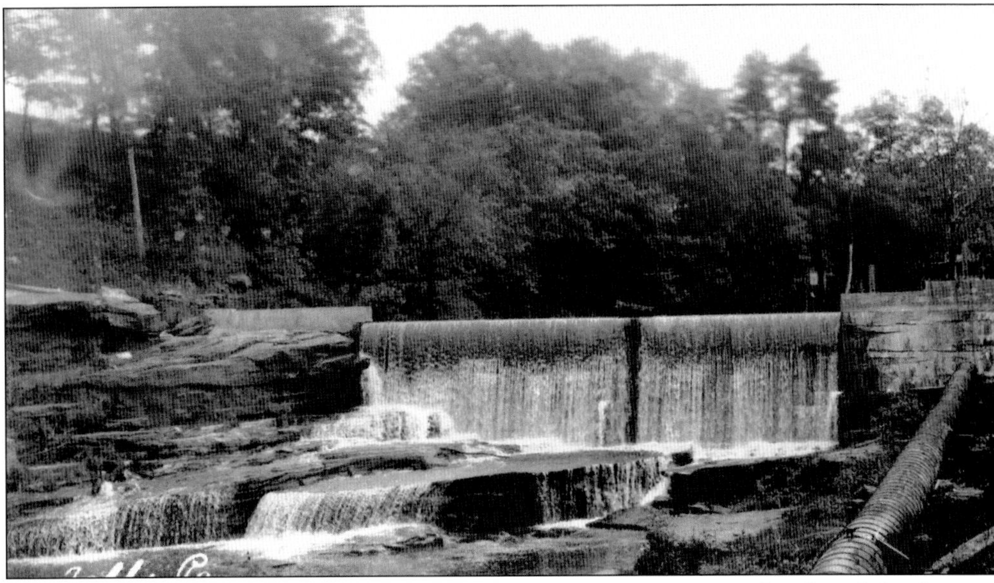

The elevation change made Falls a good place to operate a water-powered mill, and this dam was built to power it. The water pipe going to the mill can be seen on the right side of the view.

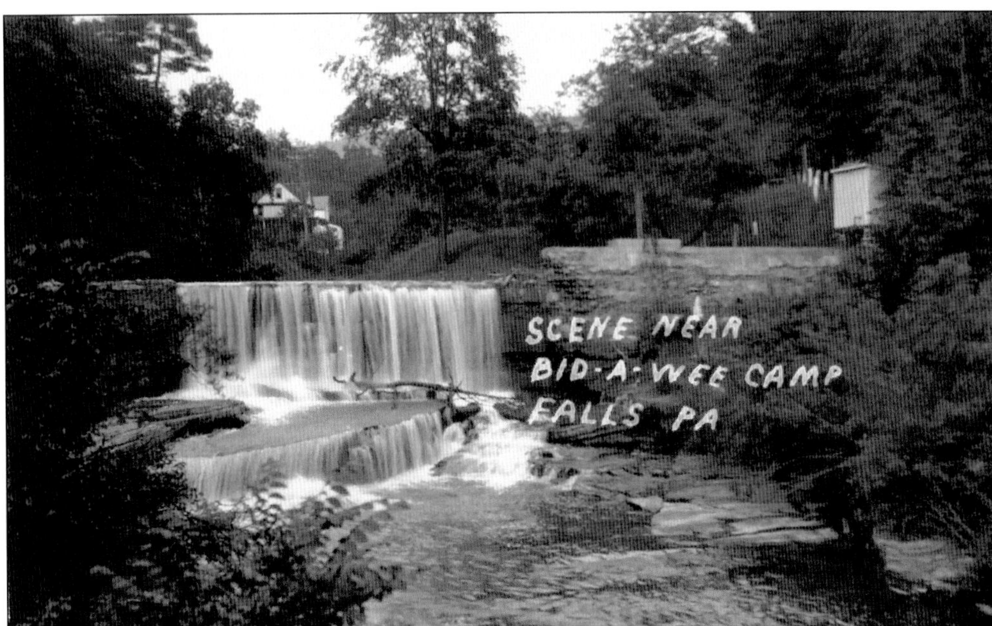

This postcard notes that the dam at Falls is "near Bid-A-Wee Camp."

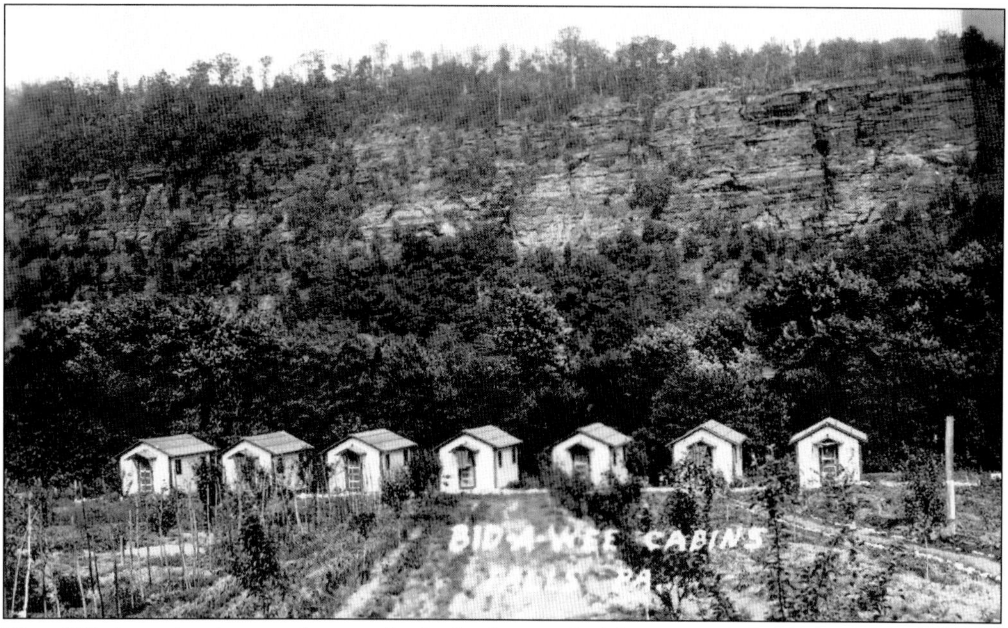

The cliffs along the river can be seen in the background of this view of the Bid-A-Wee Cabins at Falls. The cabins were located on the Exeter Township side of the river.

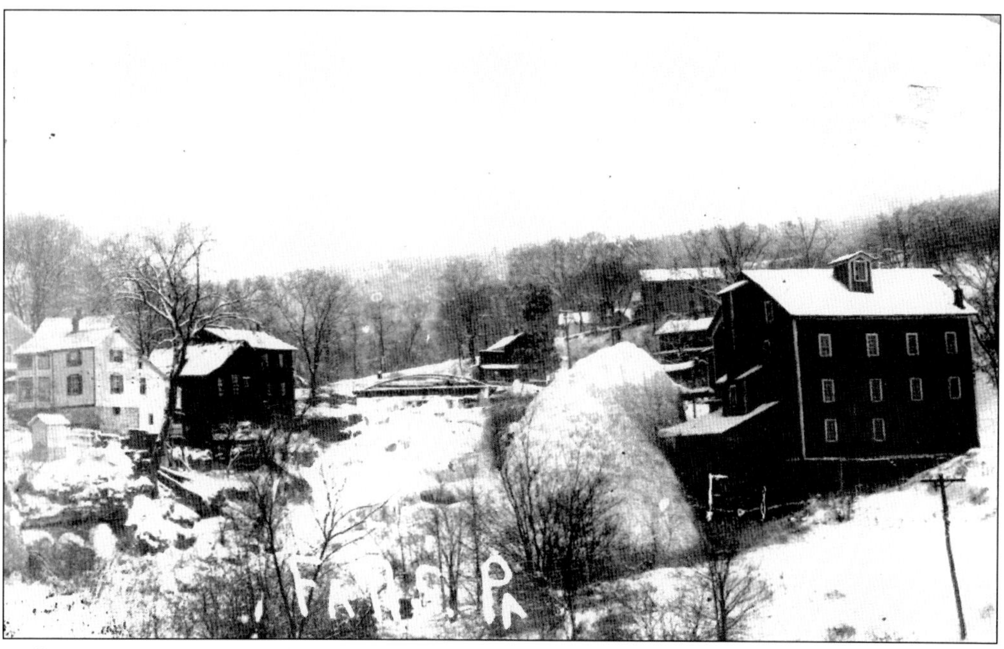

Mills were started in the Falls area in the early 1800s. Notice the ice next to the mill.

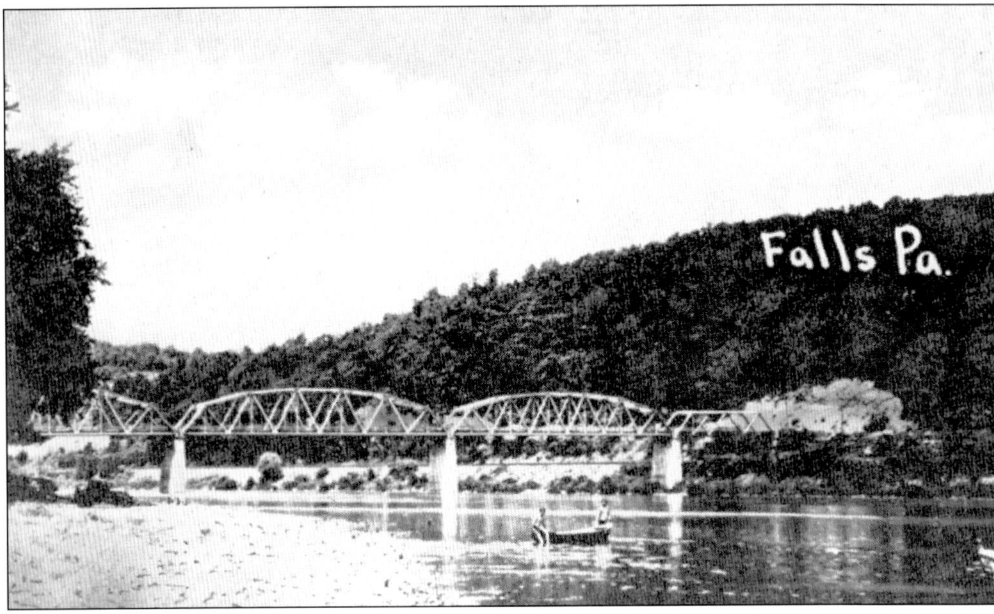

The bridge across the Susquehanna River in Falls was built between 1919 and 1921 and was in use until the 1990s, when it was replaced by the current concrete bridge.

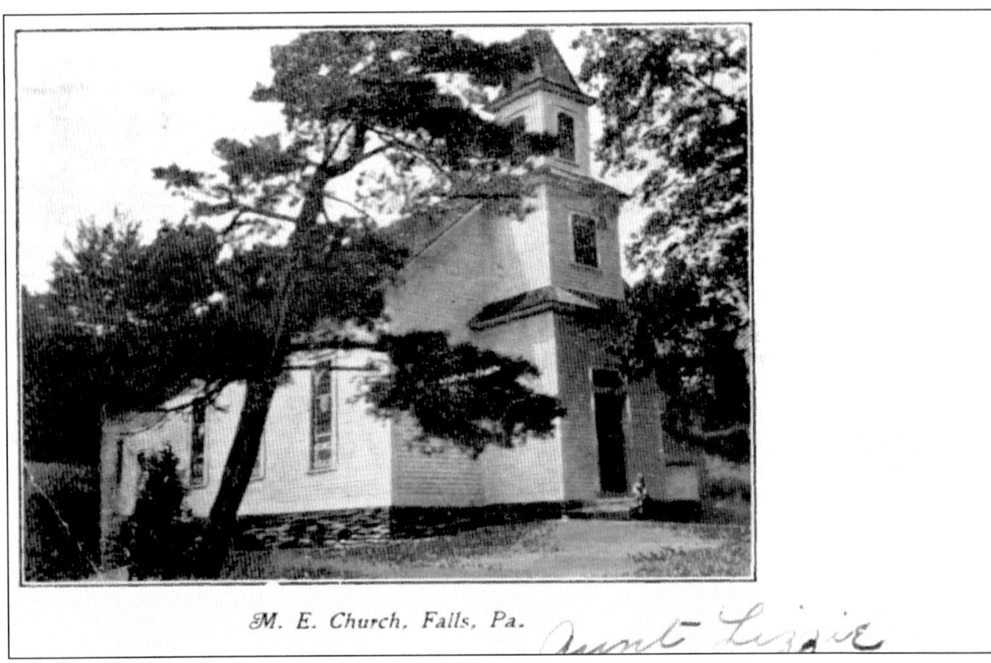

An addition was constructed on the rear of the Methodist Episcopal church in Falls after this postcard was mailed in 1907.

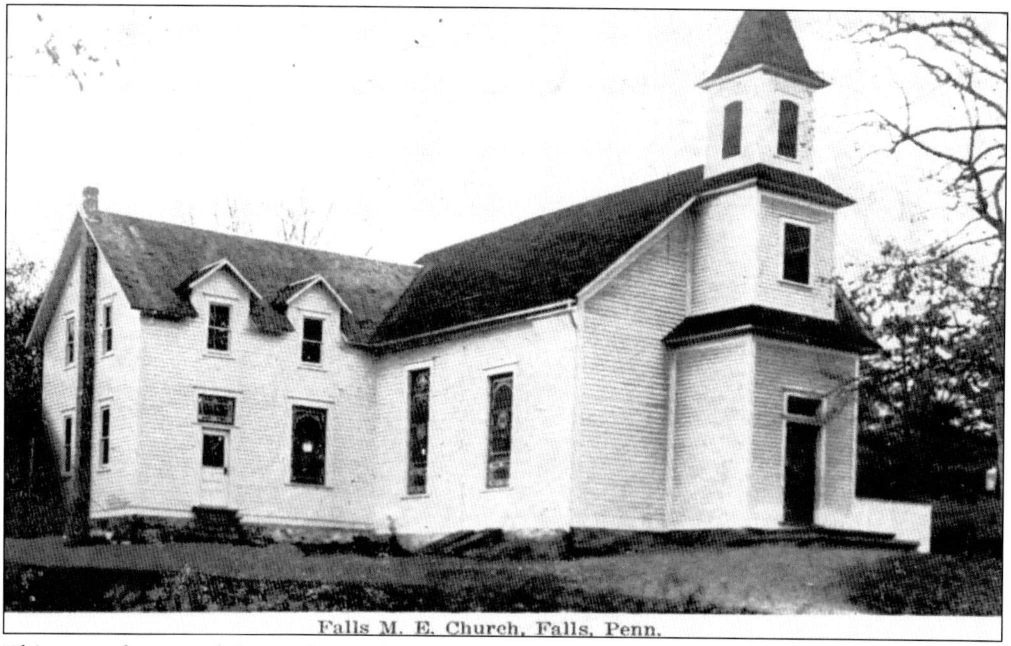

This unused postcard shows the Methodist Episcopal church with the addition.

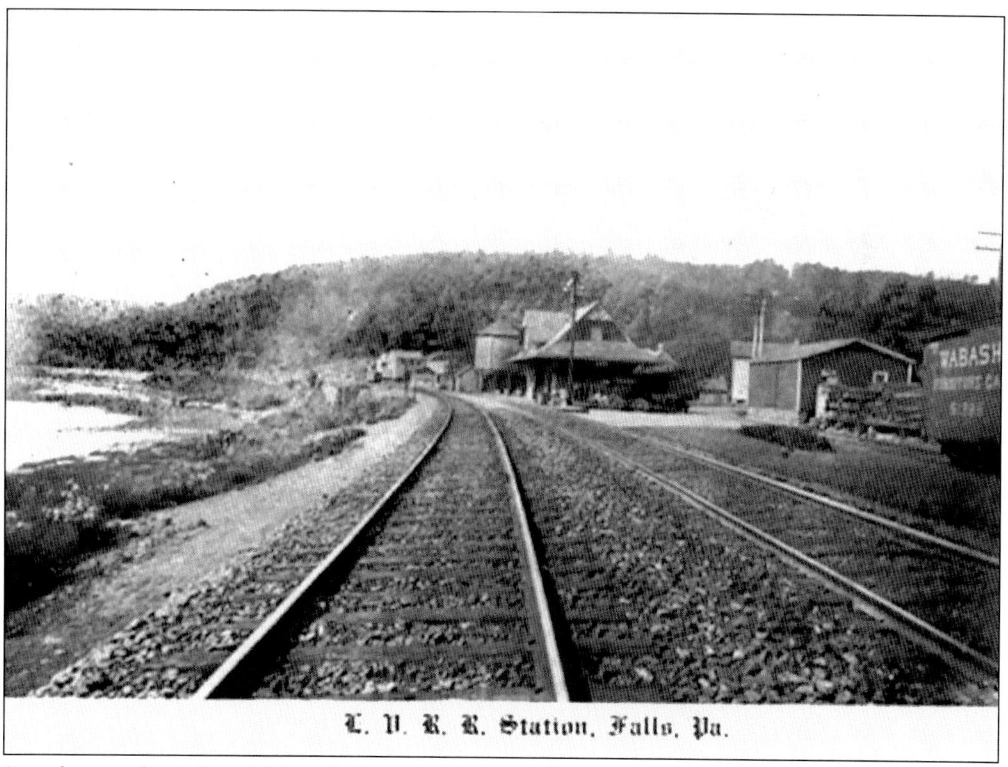

Seen here is the Lehigh Valley Railroad station in Falls.

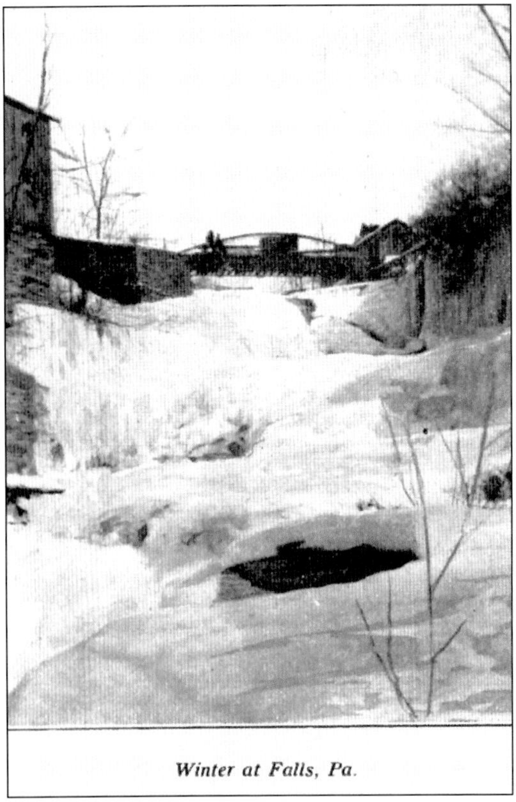

Ice and snow cover the water in this view of the winter at Falls, looking up from the area of the mill toward the milldam.

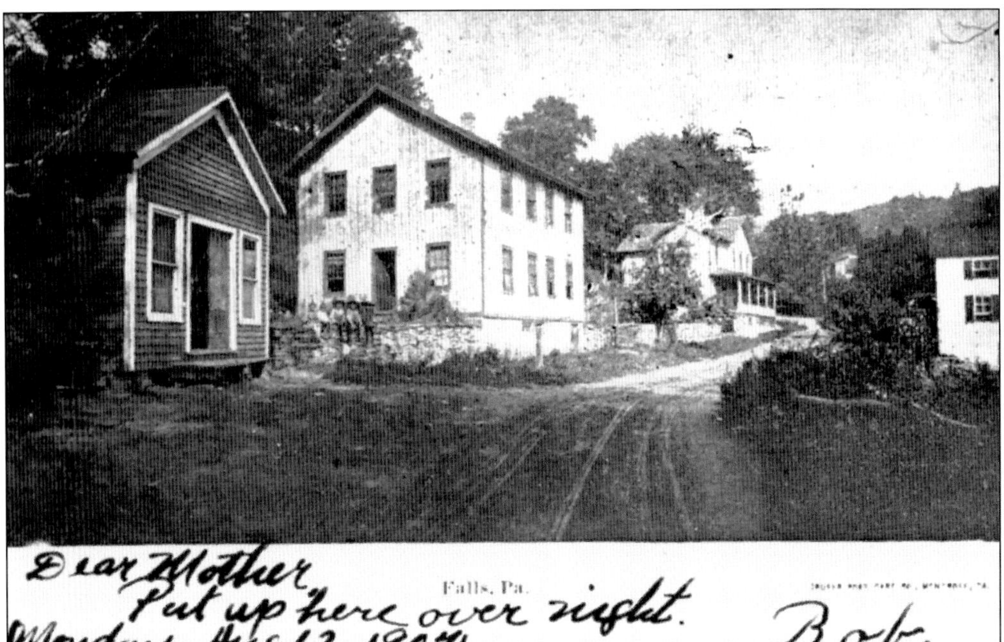

This is how the town of Falls looked in the early 1900s.

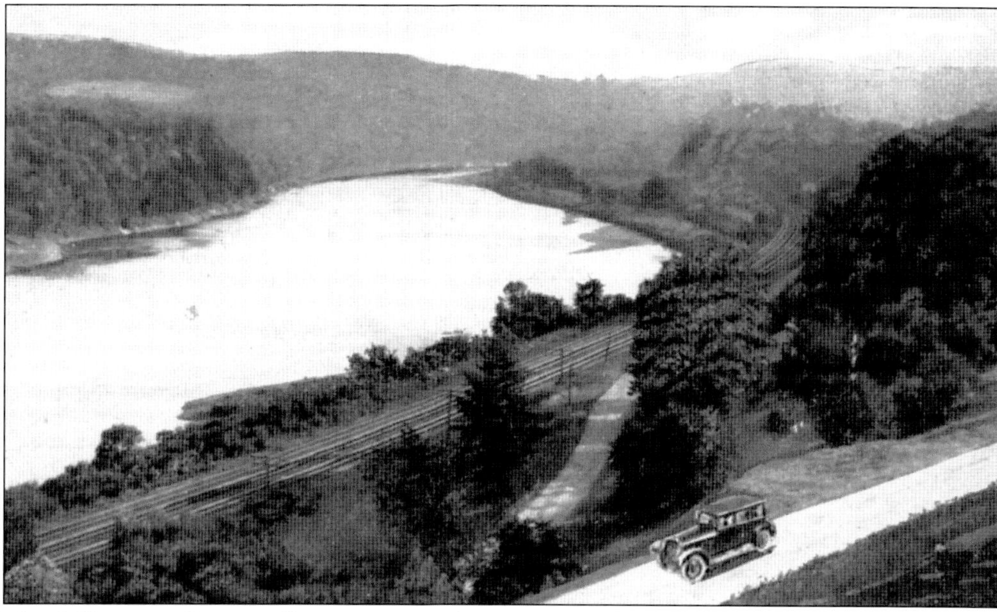

The Sullivan Trail near Falls was named after Gen. John Sullivan. He and his troops marched through Wyoming County from Easton on his way to the Iroquois Territory in New York to retaliate for the 1778 Wyoming Massacre.

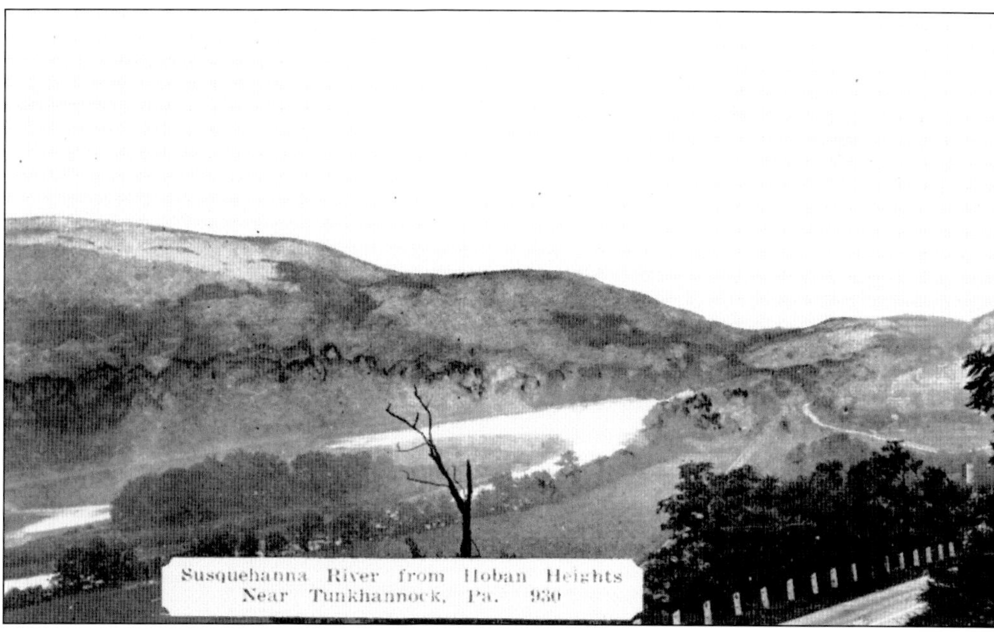

The area now known as Hoban Heights was originally called White's Ferry after the ferry service located there. The name was changed in 1927 by the Post Office Department.

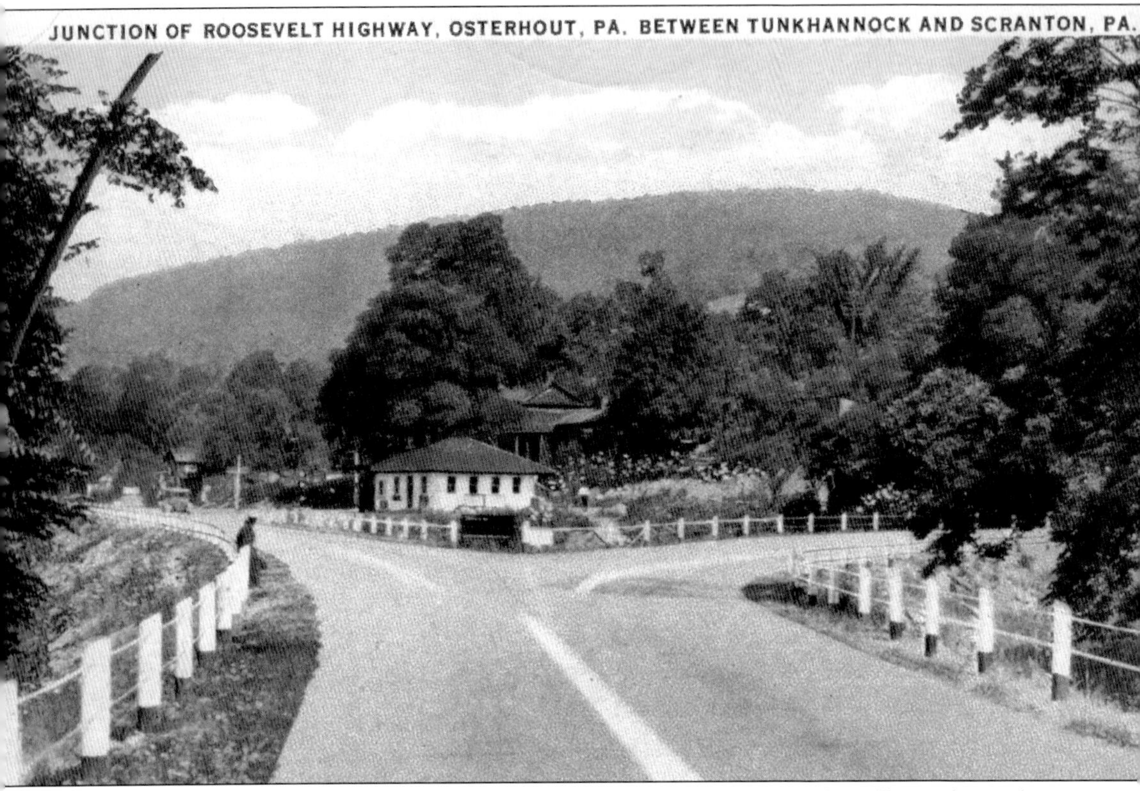

The building shown here, at the intersection Routes 92 and 307 in the village of Osterhout, is now home to Triangle Auto. This card is postmarked 1928.

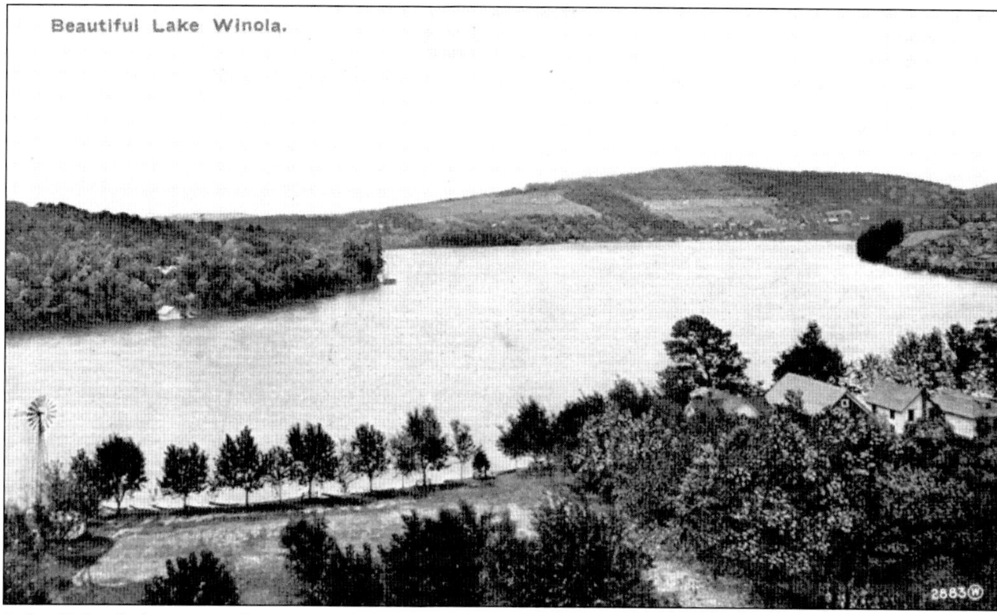

Lake Winola has served as a resort area for the local cities since the late 1800s.

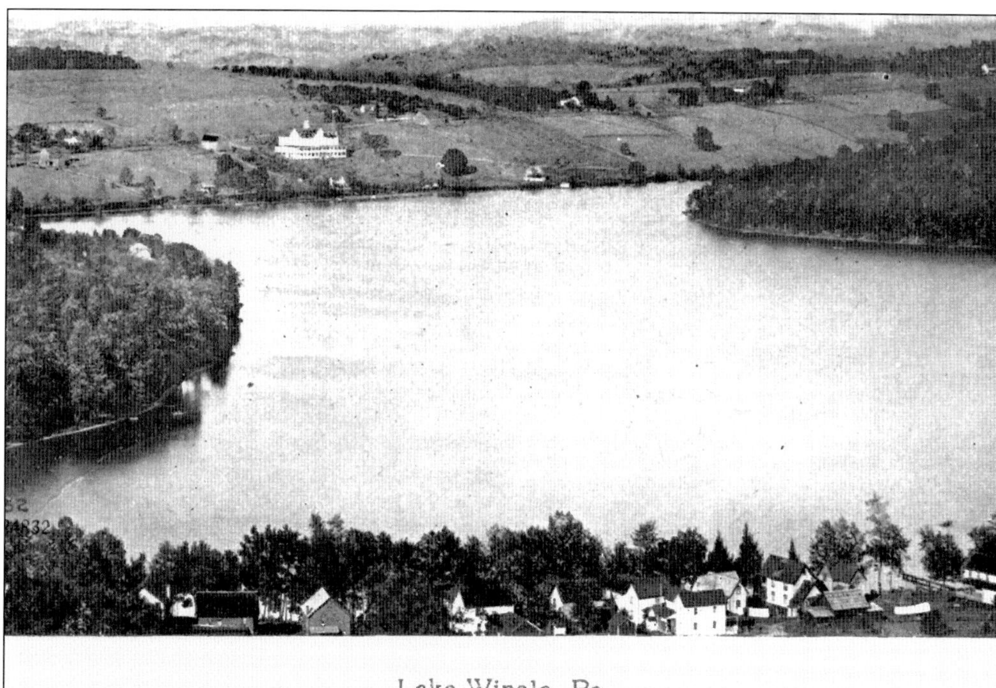

Lake Winola became even more popular after 1905, when the Northern Electric Street Railway reached the lake. The railway was a trolley system that operated from Scranton to Montrose.

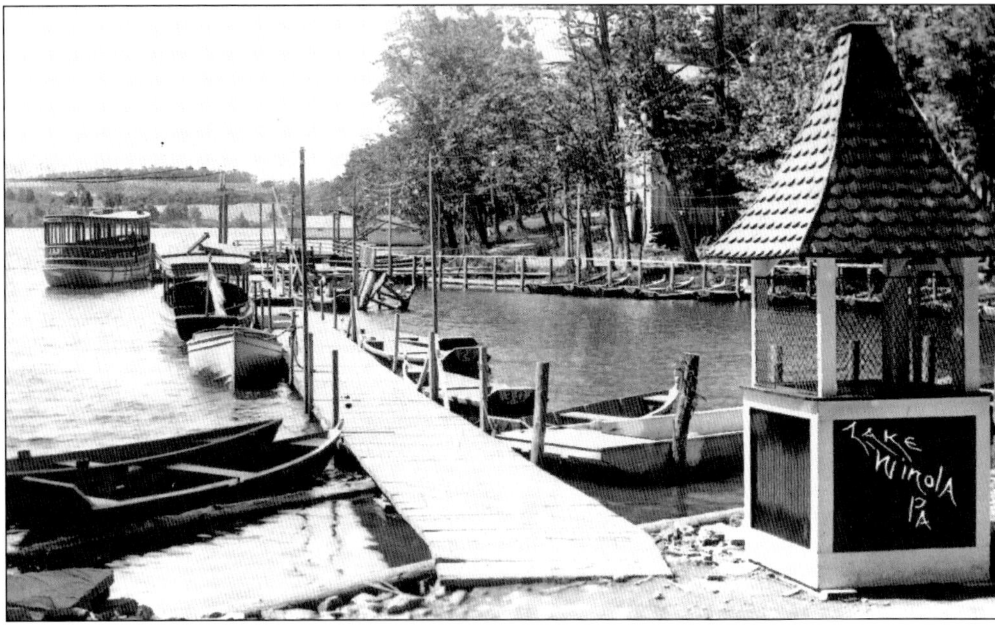

Boating was a popular pastime on Lake Winola.

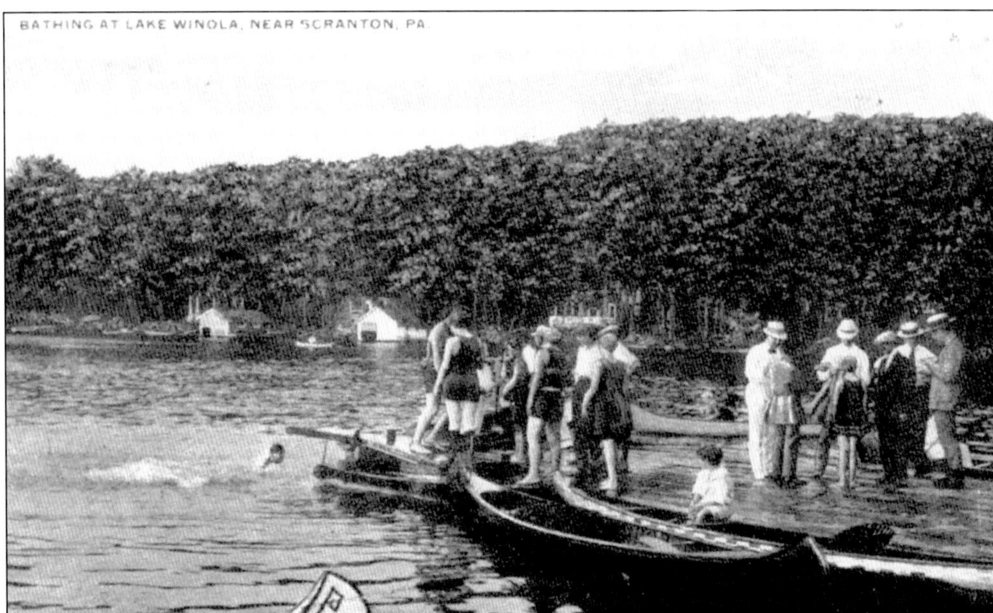

Lake Winola became a perfect spot for swimming—or as it was known, "bathing."

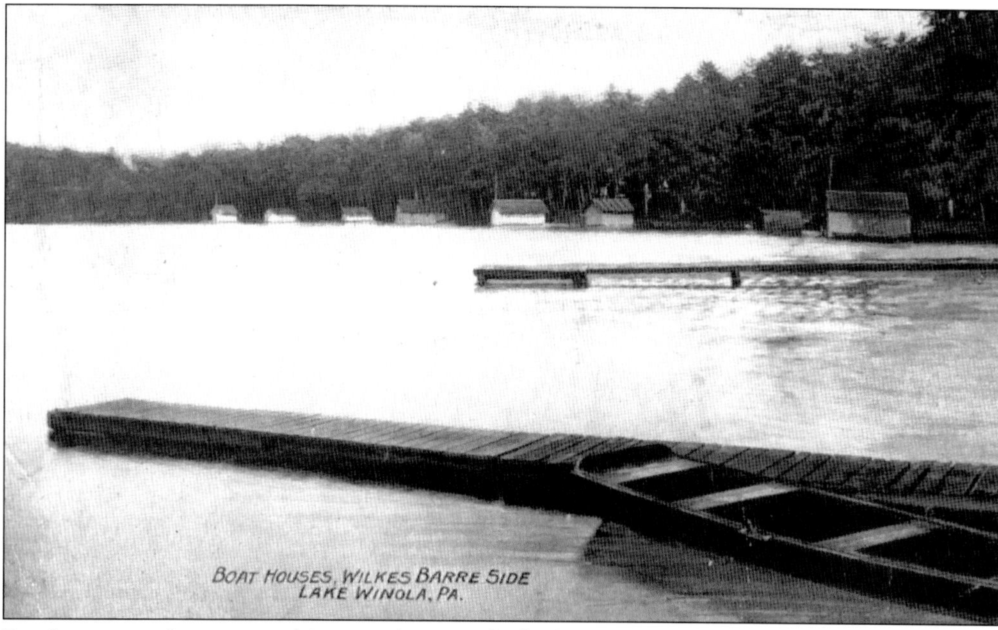

Boathouses can be seen on this unused postcard of Lake Winola.

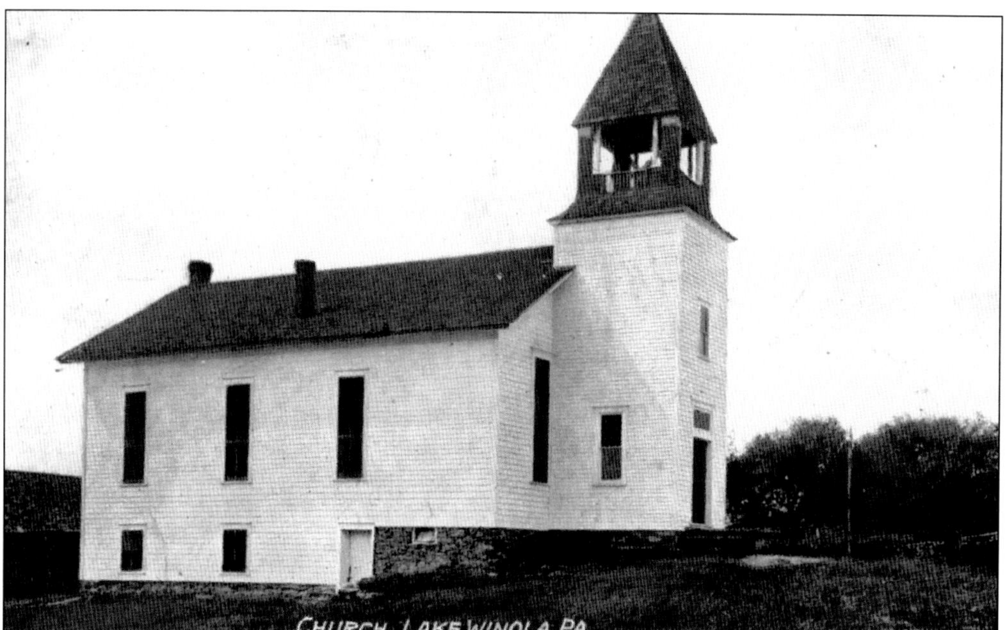

The Lake Winola Methodist Church was dedicated in 1871.

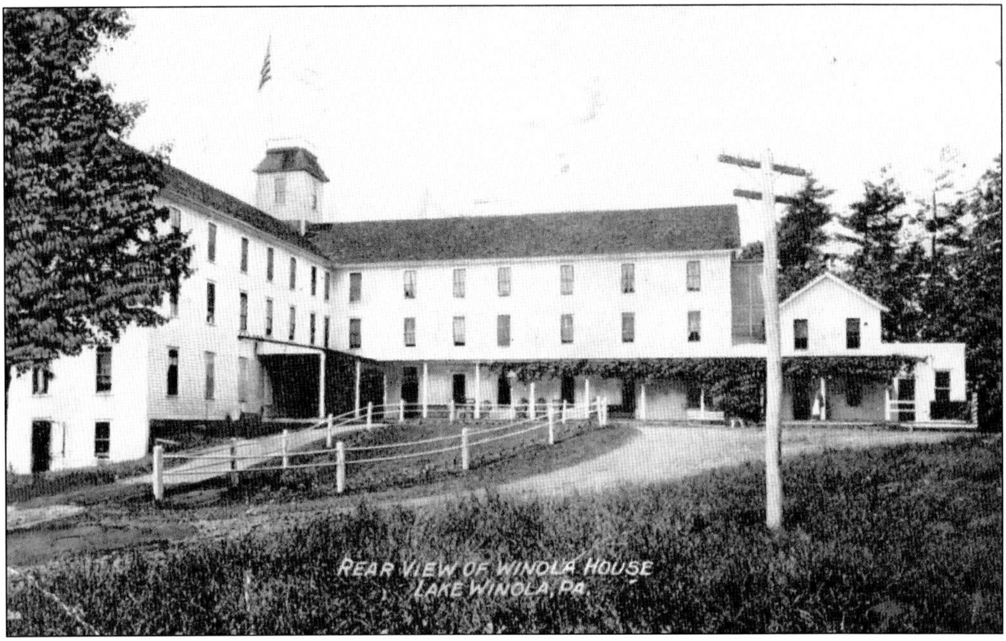

The Winola House, shown here from behind, was built in 1885 by Clark Frear. The hotel burned in 1905. The building was replaced but burned again in the 1980s.

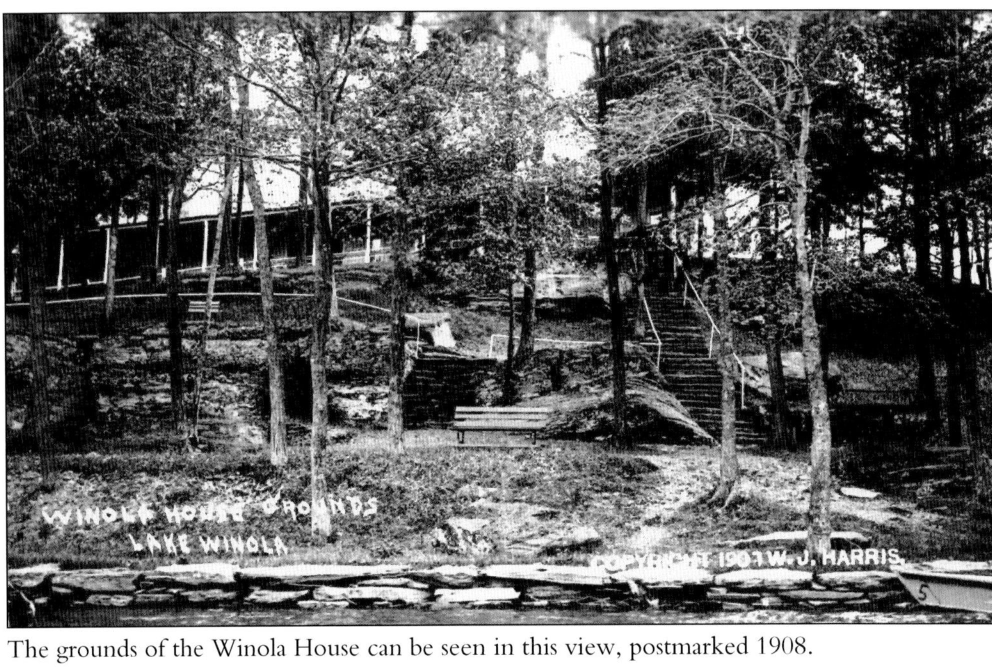

The grounds of the Winola House can be seen in this view, postmarked 1908.

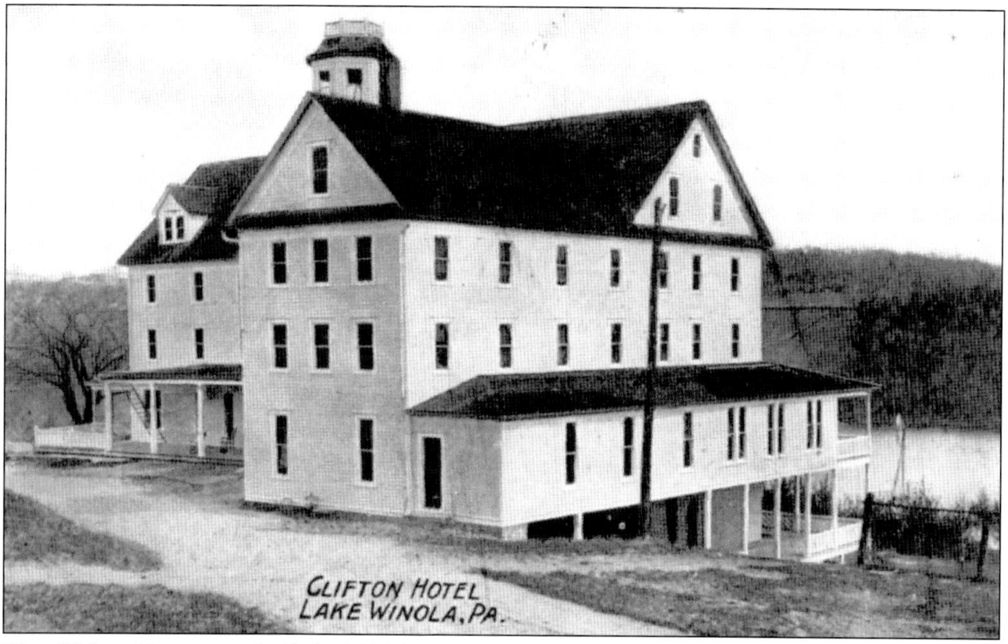

The Clifton House was built in 1903 by James W. Moore on the east side of Lake Winola and suffered the same fate as the Winola House, burning in 1922.

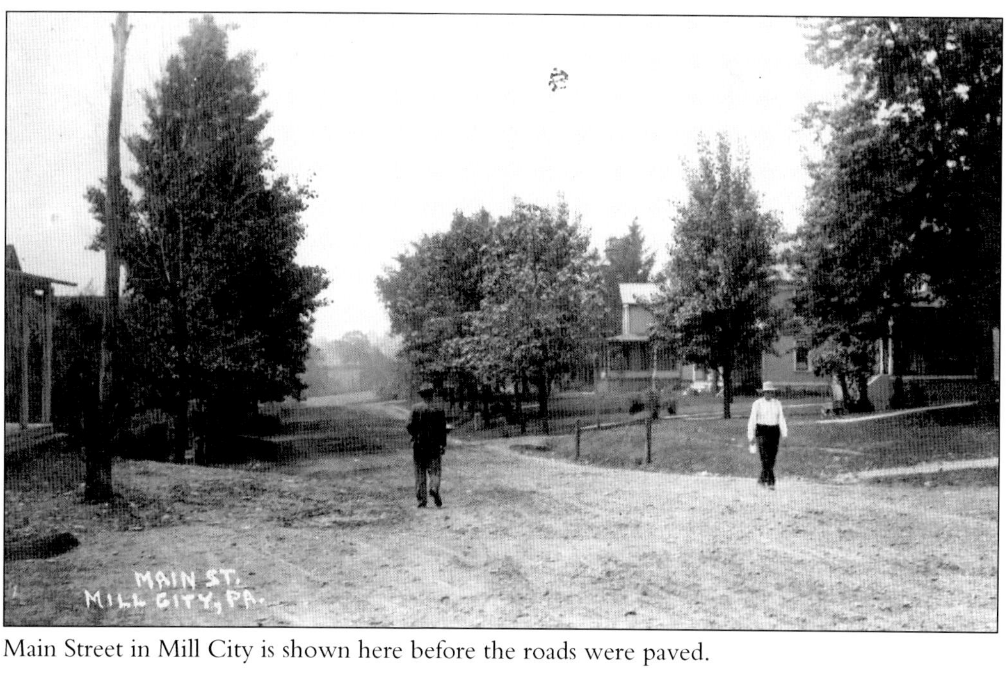

Main Street in Mill City is shown here before the roads were paved.

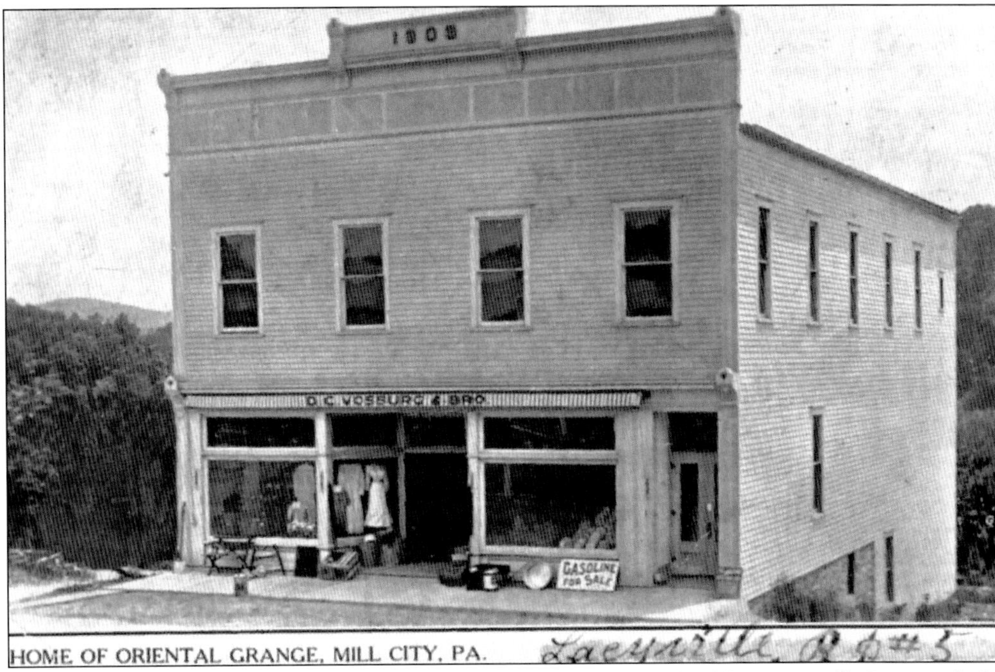

The Oriental Grange was located on the second floor of this building in Mill City, and the D. C. Vosburg & Brother store was located on the first floor. The card is postmarked 1912.

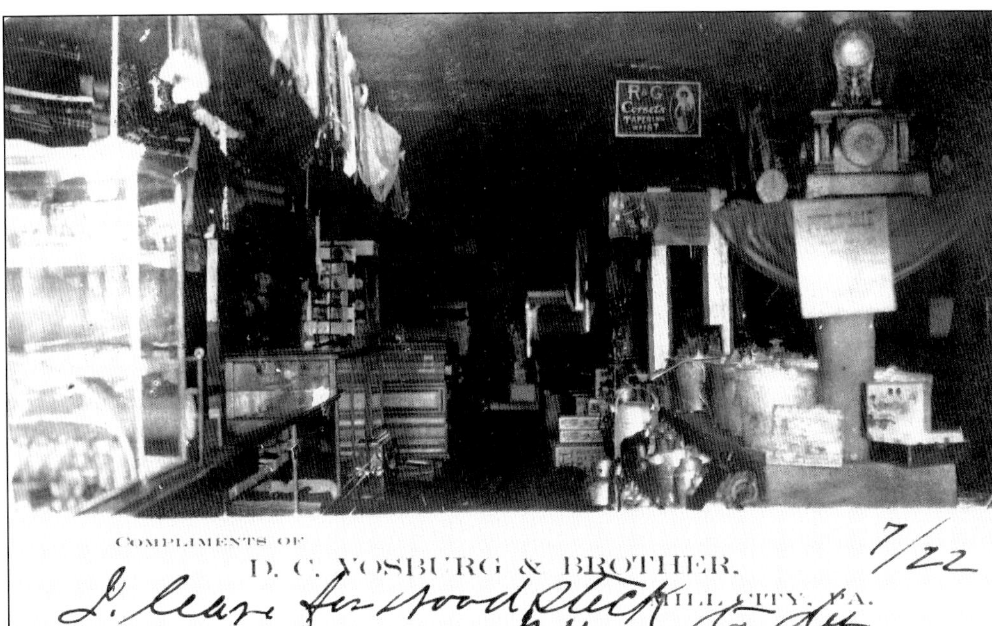

This card, postmarked 1907, shows the interior of the D. C. Vosburg & Brother store in Mill City.

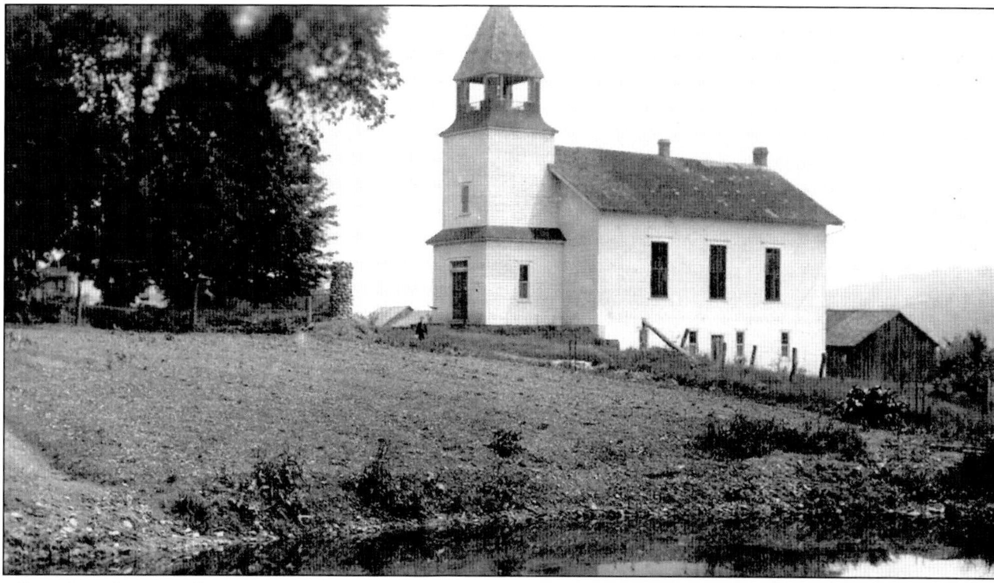
This church in Mill City is most likely the Methodist Episcopal church.

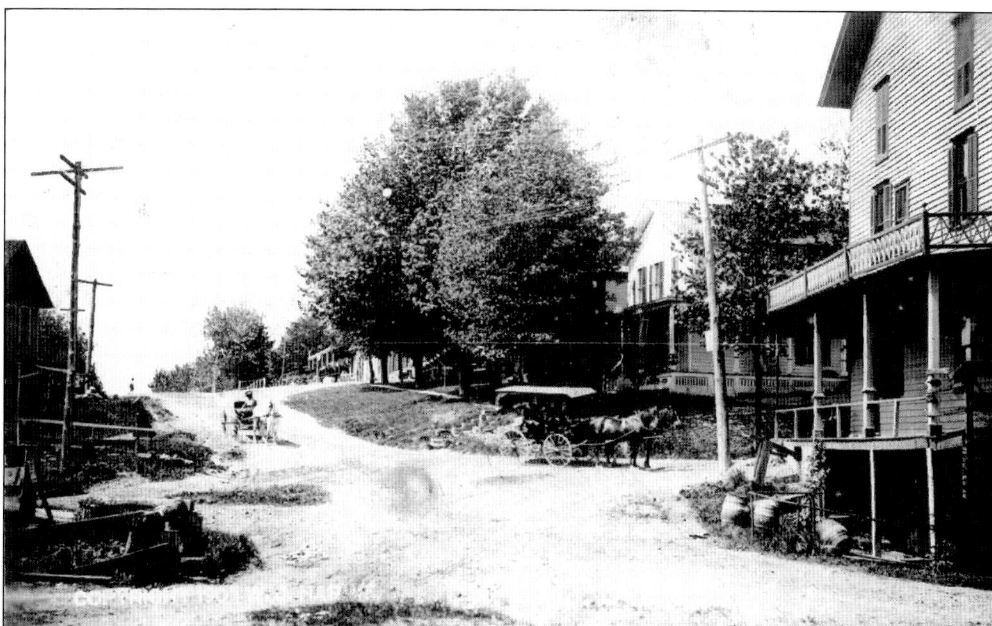
This card shows Mill City as it looked in 1908.

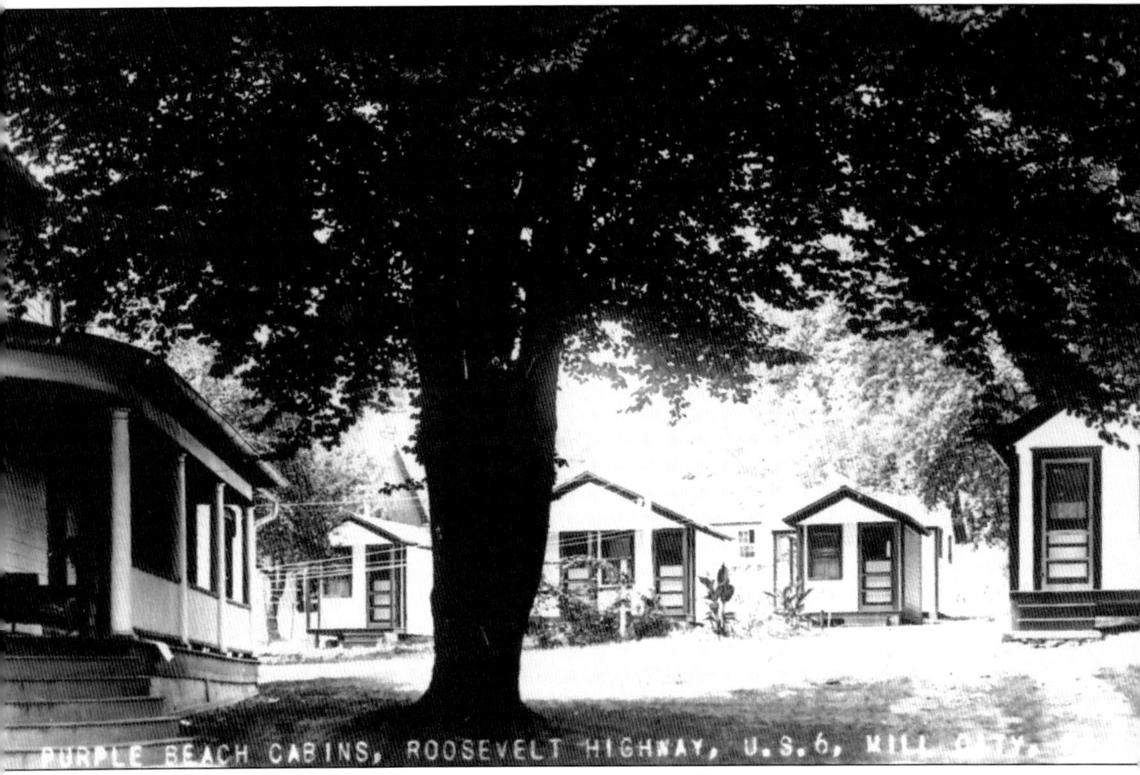

The Purple Beach Cabins were located on Route 6 in Mill City.